FRANCES RIDLEY HAVERGAL:
A Poet for the King

EILEEN M. BERRY

journey forth ®

Greenville, South Carolina

Library of Congress Cataloging-in Publication Data
Names: Berry, Eileen M., 1970- author.
Title: Frances Ridley Havergal : a poet for the king / Eileen M. Berry.
Description: Greenville, South Carolina : JourneyForth, [2019] | Audience:
    Ages: 9-12. | Audience: Grades: 4-6. | Includes bibliographical
    references.
Identifiers: LCCN 2019004913 (print) | LCCN 2019012620 (ebook) | ISBN
    9781628566857 (e-book) | ISBN 9781628566840 (pbk. : alk. paper)
Subjects: LCSH: Havergal, Frances Ridley, 1836-1879—Juvenile literature. |
    Hymn writers—England—Biography—Juvenile literature. | Women poets,
    English—Biography—Juvenile literature.
Classification: LCC PR4759.H8 (ebook) | LCC PR4759.H8 Z54 2019
(print) | DDC
    828/.809 [B] —dc23
LC record available at https://lccn.loc.gov/2019004913

All Scripture is quoted from the King James Version.

Illustrations by Del Thompson
Design by Elly Kalagayan
Page layout by Michael Boone

© 2019 BJU Press
Greenville, South Carolina 29609
JourneyForth Books is a division of BJU Press.

ISBN 978-1-62856-684-0
eISBN 978-1-62856-685-7

15   14   13   12   11   10   9   8   7   6   5   4   3   2   1

*With appreciation to Dawn and Jamie
for honing my craft as teachers,
offering your wisdom as colleagues,
and gracing my life as friends.*

CONTENTS

Author's Note   vii

For There We Sing   1

A Thorn amid the Flowers   10

A Moaning in the Music   20

Peace Is Made   32

Truehearted, Wholehearted   42

Tender Lambs   55

In Thy Service Glad and Free   65

Darkest Hour Is Nearest Dawning   74

Some Mountain Days   85

Ever, Only, All for Thee   90

Every Joy or Trial   96

I Could Not Do Without Thee   106

Take What Thou Wilt   114

I Am Trusting Thee, Lord Jesus   124

Epilogue   129

Sources   131

AUTHOR'S NOTE

Open nearly any English hymnal today, and Frances Ridley Havergal's name will appear on several of its pages. Havergal was one of the foremost English hymn writers of her time. Among her hymns still in use today are "Take My Life and Let It Be," "Like a River Glorious," "I Gave My Life for Thee," and "Who Is on the Lord's Side?" Her hymns, poems, and other works have been translated into multiple languages, including Russian and Arabic.

Although she left this legacy of enduring hymns, her story is rarely told. Her life is easily overlooked because it was unremarkable in many ways. She lived to be only forty-two years of age. She was not a foreign missionary or the leader of a great movement. She never married or had children of her own. She was often in ill health. Her social sphere was confined to a limited circle of family, friends, and acquaintances. And yet God used her writings in powerful ways for His glory. By the end of her life, she had received so many letters from those her work had touched that she could not answer them all. How did a sheltered Victorian woman become so widely known and used of God?

Perhaps the answer lies in one deep, defining quality of her life: consecration. Havergal would have been the first to admit that she was not perfect. But she was devoted to her Savior, and her earnest desire in every area of life was to be useful to Him. Christ had her heart, and because of that He had everything else—her time, her energies, her talents, her finances, and her relationships. No matter where she went or what she was doing, she had a constant sense of her Lord's ownership over her life.

Frances Ridley Havergal's story deserves to be told. It shows that consecration to Jesus Christ is possible through the ordinary moments of everyday life. I have chosen to tell her story in free verse as I imagine she might have told it, with her poetry woven throughout. Every incident is based on information recorded in her journals and letters or in the words of her biographers. In the interest of engaging young readers, some of the details and conversations are imagined.

FOR THERE WE SING

1

"Flora, wait for me!" I race after the spaniel,
  laughing at the way her long ears flap
  like wings when she runs.
*Naughty Flo. She knows I can't chase her
  through the hedge.*

The white wagging tail disappears
  beneath holly bushes, neatly trimmed.

I groan and sink down on the grass.
  "I'll make up a song about you, naughty dog."

I gaze up past the garden wall to where
  the wooded hills rise,
    wearing their spring dress of golden green.

I love these hills.

For as long as I can remember, my family and I have
  lived here.
The English country air is the air
  I've always breathed.
My first five years were spent in the Astley Rectory;
  then we moved here to Hallow, to Henwick House.

The garden is my favorite place in the world.
From my seat near the hedge, I can see the first
  slender green shoots, daffodils springing up.
I helped Mamma plant them last year.

Now for a song. *Hmmm.*
What kind of song does one sing to a dog?
I hum a few notes and begin to sing.

  I shall find you, naughty Flo.
  Through the hedge you mustn't go.

I jump up and stand on tiptoe. I'm not quite tall enough
  to see over the hedge. I'm afraid to get too close to the
  prickly holly.
I stoop down to peer under the bush. Beneath it I can
  just see
    Flora's nose moving about, sniffing
    the empty flower beds.

  If you wander far away . . .

I pause and hum the ending of the tune. I hum it again.

If you wander far away . . .

Now a strong voice sings out the missing words from
   just behind me.

"I will bring you home, I say."

Papa! I whirl around. "Papa, you surprised me."

"Making up songs again, my little songbird?"

Papa scoops me up and I am high above the world,
   so high I can see Flo trotting along on the other side
   of the hedgerow.
I wrap my arm around Papa's neck.

"Flo ran through the hedge, and I can't reach her, Papa."
From my perch I point down at the little dog.
"She's over in the church flower beds
   where I'm not supposed to play."

"I'll go out through the gate and get her," says Papa.
"Wait right here." He sets me down and heads
   for the gate.
Peering through the holly, I watch the chase.
Oh, what a glorious game it is for Flo!
Papa whistles and claps, trying to herd the dog back
   through the gate.
Flora leaps and dodges, her tongue hanging out,
   her long, silky ears bouncing.
She is the happiest dog in the world.

I double over with giggles.

Papa glances toward the hedge.
"Call her, Fanny. I've got her headed to the gate."

I jump up and whistle long and loud. "Here, Flo.
  Come, Flo!"

A moment later the little dog rounds the corner,
  running toward me full speed. I grab the wriggling,
  panting bundle of fur.
Flo licks my face with wet doggy kisses.
I try to be angry. "Naughty Flo!"
But I am smiling.

Papa comes back through the gate.
"I'll have the gardener close up the hole.
She won't be able to go through it again.
Now come inside, Fanny. I have something to show you."

Papa leads the way to the pianoforte
  in the rectory parlor.
"I've finished another psalm setting," he tells me.

"Oh, Papa, will you teach it to me?"

"Of course. I would very much like to have your opinion
  on it."

I love the way his eyes twinkle with fun
  and the way he talks to me as if I am all grown up.
Papa knows how I love to sit on the bench beside him,
  swinging my legs, listening to him play the music he
  writes for church.

Papa spreads out some pages with notes and words
  carefully penciled in.
"I've decided to use a major key this time," he says,
  "to go with Sunday's message about Psalm 103.
Not a melancholy psalm by any means. You'll like
  the melody, I think.

A lilting tune that will suit your soprano voice well."
He winks at me and begins to play the introduction.

"Sing it too, Papa. I want to hear the words
   with the tune."

Papa's voice rings out, singing words from the
   Scottish psalter
   to the new tune he has written. I watch his long
fingers dance over the keys, bringing the scribblings
on the page into joyful life.

O thou my soul, bless God the Lord;
And all that in me is
Be stirred up His holy name
To magnify and bless.

2

I was born Frances Ridley Havergal
   in England on December 14, 1836.
My nickname was Fanny among my family.
The Ridley part of my name was after a family friend.
But I always liked to remember
   that Ridley was also the name of an English minister,
   a martyr who had died for his Christian faith.

I suppose I was a little spoiled as the baby of the family.
I was blessed with a bright mind
   and a good memory, and I could learn quickly.
My health was too fragile
   for me to go to school till later in my childhood.
My older sister Miriam became my tutor.

They tell me I could speak clearly and fluently
  by the age of two
  and could read easy books at three years old.
I remember how I loved stories. It wasn't unusual
  for Mamma to find me hiding under the table
  with a storybook in my hands,
  lost in another time and place as I read.

By four years old I could read the Bible and write
  on my own.
I did not know at the time how greatly those two loves,
  the Bible and writing,
  would become a part of me.

I loved the outdoors.
How happy for me that my father, a rector
  in the Church of England,
  had country parishes when I was young.
I was much younger than my other siblings,
  and I sometimes had no one to play with.
Time alone with the waving branches of trees
  and the warm sunlight
  taught me to be thoughtful.
I often thought about God, the Creator of all the beauty
  I saw around me.

My constant companion in those early years was the
  family dog,
  a white and tan spaniel named Flora.
Flo and I were the same age.
How I loved to run after Flo on a breezy day,
  feeling the wind in my face,
  or climb trees while she barked up at me from below.

3

My first great grief came when Flo died.
I was seven years old.
I hid in the garden while Papa dug the burial hole.
We had chosen the spot together
  beneath a small tree with white, star-shaped flowers.
My tears dripped onto the paper
  where I wrote this epitaph:

Here lies little Flora.
Died April 16th, 1844.
Aged 7.
Reverence her remains.

Papa called me when the hole was ready.
He had placed Flora's small body in a little box,
  and I laid my paper on the lid.
Together we sang a hymn,
  our voices thin and shaky in the wind.
Then I watched his shovel piling the dirt on top,
  watched until the scene became a watery blur.

We stood by the little mound in silence then,
  Papa holding my hand and giving it gentle squeezes
  till my fingers stopped their trembling.

4

Papa was the sun in my sky.
I always sat on his knee in the morning at family prayers,
  listening to his calm, musical voice read the Bible.
Music was his gift and his passion.

Often he composed hymn tunes to be sung
    at our church.
It was he who taught me to sing hymns.

Growing up in a home filled with music,
    I learned early to love singing, music, and poetry.
Even as a very young child I made up songs and rhymes.
I filled a little notebook with my poems and stories.

5

I open the creaky wooden drawer of my bedside table
    with a new poem fluttering around inside me
    like one of those butterflies in the garden.
I pull out my notebook
    and the stubby pencil I keep beside it.
Out in the hall I crawl into my favorite spot
    in the shadows under the table
    where I can watch the feet go by and
    where I can be so quiet
    that people sometimes walk by never knowing
    I am here.

I must write down the poem,
    must capture it on paper before it slips away.
I thought it out in church today.
It's my best one yet. And it will help me remember
    that Sunday is the most important day of the week,
    like Papa always says.

I flip through the pages
    filled with story ideas, drawings,
    and unfinished rhymes.
On the first blank page I write my new rhyme
    from memory,

scribbling as fast as I can,
the way I would net the butterfly with one quick swoop.
Then I put down my pencil
and read over my round lettering.

> *Sunday is a pleasant day,*
> *When we to church do go;*
> *For there we sing and read and pray,*
> *And hear the sermon too.*
>
> *On Sunday hear the village bells;*
> *It seems as if they said,*
> *Go to the church where the pastor tells*
> *How Christ for man has bled.*
>
> *And if we love to pray and read*
> *While we are in our youth,*
> *The Lord will help us in our need*
> *And keep us in His truth.*

For there we sing.
Yes, if the truth be known, what I like best about church
is the singing.
Not the reading and the praying.

I sigh. I wish the Lord would help me.
I know it's all true, what Papa says from the pulpit,
what he reads from the big Bible each morning.
But I don't think
I have the new heart Papa speaks of.
I don't believe I love God as I ought.
I suppose I should have been listening to the sermon
instead of writing this poem in my head.

I'm just as naughty as Flora.
Maybe if I pray and read the Bible a little more,
I'll do better.

A THORN AMID
THE FLOWERS

1

I stand at the window
  in my new room in the house in Worcester.
It is so different here.
There are no gardens, no trees and flowers,
  only carriages in the street below
  and rooftops stretching all the way to the horizon.

The only bit of beauty I can see from the window
  is a tiny patch of sky.
It is now sunset, and a purple cloud
  swims in the little sea of pink between rooftops.

"Fanny."

Papa speaks gently from the doorway, and I turn.

"You are like a little caged lark here.
I fear I shall never hear my songbird sing again.
Can you not be happy?"

My eyes fill with tears. "Oh, Papa,
I know you like being rector
  of the new St. Nicholas church.

But I miss so many things about the country.
I miss the gardens, the holly, the daffodils, the trees,
    especially the tree where Flora is buried."

Papa comes to stand behind me,
    to look over my shoulder at the little purple cloud.
He places a hand on my shoulder.
"But you will find things to love here too.
Worcester is a place of history.
Grand cathedrals, Tudor architecture, old battlefields.
Think of it!
And you have a room of your own
    where you may read and write to your heart's content.
Look at your view of the sunset.
What a lovely place to pray."

And then softly he quotes the psalm
   he read at family prayers this morning.

"My voice shalt thou hear in the morning, O Lord;
   in the morning will I direct my prayer unto thee,
   and will look up."

I turn away from the window.
I do not feel like talking about prayer.

"How is Mamma?
She didn't come down to tea.
I haven't seen her all afternoon."

Papa's face clouds like the winter sky.
"Your mother is very tired, Fanny.
She is taking her tea in bed.
When she is finished, you may go in to see her.
I'm sure that would cheer her up.
Why don't you think of a song you could sing for her?"

I gaze up at the wrinkles that line his forehead
   like furrows in a farmer's field
   back home in the countryside.
He is worried about Mamma.
"I'll go to her in a few minutes, Papa."
For his sake I make myself smile.
"I shall sing her one of my new songs."

I tiptoe softly to my mother's room
   and knock on the door.

"Come in, dear."
Mamma's voice is faint and breathy, like a sigh.

My older sister, Maria, is just leaving
   with Mamma's tray.

"Fanny, Mamma needs to rest.
Perhaps you ought to come back later."

But Mamma holds out her hand to me.
"I will see my little girl now."

I walk over to the bed and take Mamma's hand.
"Would you like to hear my new song, Mamma?
It's about the little patch of sky I can see
   from my room."

Mamma's answer is a smile, so I begin.
I watch Mamma's eyes while I sing,
   hoping to see their sparkle return.
Mamma looks so weak and tired.

"That was a lovely song, Fanny,"
   she says when I am finished.

"Mamma, I'm sure you'll get better soon.
Perhaps we'll all go to church together next Sunday."

"Perhaps. Now, dear, go downstairs
   and play and sing some hymns for me while I rest."

"Yes, Mamma."
I lean down to kiss her
   and then hurry downstairs to the piano.

2

After the move to the St. Nicholas Rectory in Worcester,
   I lost my happy spirit.
It wasn't just that I missed my home in the country.

I had another deep trouble
  I could tell to no one.

I wanted to be a Christian like my parents,
  but I knew that I was not.
I had grown up in a pastor's home,
  had heard God's Word all my life.
I knew how a true Christian should feel and act.
But for me it wasn't real.
I did not love God.
Instead, I felt frightened of Him.

I misbehaved at home. Quite often.
And I even enjoyed it sometimes.
When I tried to be good, it seemed no use.
I did not want to read the Bible and pray.
And the church services held no joy for me,
  except when we sang Papa's songs.
The sermons only made me feel guilty.
It was like struggling in a quicksand.
The more you struggle,
  the deeper you sink.

3

Dusk has fallen Sunday evening,
  and it is time to leave church and walk home.
The curate is standing by the door,
  shaking people's hands,
  smiling, laughing, saying goodnight.

But his words in the sermon he just preached
  squirm inside me like the worms
  I've watched my brothers put on their fishing hooks.

I cannot talk to Papa.
He is already walking down the path to the rectory,
   eager to check on Mamma at home.
I must stay and speak to the curate.

I hang back inside the door till the others have all gone.
Then I take a deep breath and step forward.

My voice comes out shaky and rushed.
"You told us, sir, that Jesus said, 'Fear not, little flock.'
I'm afraid I'm not one of the sheep in His flock.
I want to be one of His sheep, but
   I'm not."

I am glad for the darkness veiling my face.
He will not see the tears forming in my eyes.
I plunge on.

"The truth is, sir, I think I've gotten worse
   since we've come here to the new parish.
I—I don't care at all for Bible reading and prayer."

The curate takes my cold hand in his warm one.
"My dear child," he says,
   "don't take my sermon so much to heart.
You have had a great deal of excitement,
   packing up and moving to a new place.
You feel unhappy right now
   because you're not used to your new home.
Things will get better.
Just try to be a good child.
And remember, you must never neglect your prayers."

I open my mouth, then close it again.
I cannot answer. I cannot trust my voice.
I pull my hand away, turn, and run.

I hear him calling behind me,
  "Good night, Frances."

But even louder I hear the heavy sobs
  tearing out of my throat
  and the pounding of my feet on the path.
I will never speak with anyone about this again.
Never. No one understands.

4

Except maybe Mamma.
Yes, maybe she understands better than I thought.

The next time I visit her bedside, she pats the bed.
"Fanny, sit down here for a moment.
I have something I wish to say to you."

I perch on the high bed,
  dangling my legs over the side.
My eyes never leave Mamma's face.

"Frances, you are my littlest girl.
I feel more anxious about you than the rest.
I pray for you.
Remember, Fanny, nothing but the precious blood
  of Christ
  can make you clean and lovely in God's sight."
Mamma's hand comes slowly up to rest on my cheek.
"Remember."

"I know that, Mamma. I'll remember."

"And Fanny, there's something else.
You need to pray that God will prepare you
    for all He is preparing *for* you."

I do not understand.
Something in Mamma's face makes me cold inside.
But I do not want to tire Mamma with questions.
I sit and hold her thin white hand in mine,
    watching her face
    until the weary eyes close again.

In the hall Maria catches my arm.
"Fanny, I need to talk to you. It's about Mamma.
I'm afraid you don't understand."

"Understand what?"
I suddenly feel angry. I pull my arm away
    and frown up at Maria as hard as I can.

"Mamma is very sick, and the doctor is not sure . . .
    not sure she's going to . . ."

I stamp my foot. "That's not true!
Mamma is going to get better. I know she is.
Now leave me alone."
I run into my bedroom and slam the door.

At the window I look up at my little patch of blue sky.
White, fluffy clouds are floating up there.
I watch them till the pounding of my heart slows.
But my thoughts will not rest.
What did Mamma mean?
What does God need to prepare me for?
What is God preparing for me?

5

Shortly after this conversation, my mother died.
I was eleven years old when I stood once more
   at my window,
      watching the funeral procession on its way
      to the churchyard.
I felt numb. I could not even cry.

So this was what Mamma wanted God to prepare
   me for.

I had not wanted to believe it.
I did not want to think Mamma was going to her
   "mansion in the sky,"
      as one of the church hymns put it.
Maria and Mamma and Papa had all tried to tell me.
But I had not listened. I had let myself think only
   that Mamma would get better.
But now Mamma was gone.

I always looked back on Mamma's death
   as the greatest sorrow of my childhood.
Six years afterwards, I wrote a poem about it.
I thought of the happy times I played in the garden.
And I thought of Mamma's death
   as a shadow crossing the sunlit rows of flowers,
   as a thorn that pierced my hand when I picked a rose.

> *One eclipse hath shadowed o'er my childhood's*
> *   sunny hours,*
> *And now its sharpness seemeth past, that thorn*
> *   'mid many flowers.*
> *But still the saddening feeling cometh oftener*
> *   than before . . .*

And my memory loves to dwell upon the merry
  careless hours,
When I thought the world a thornless garden full
  of lovely flowers.

Mamma made a dying request of me.
She asked me to promise to think of her
  each Sunday morning when I heard the early
  church bell.
For many years I wondered why she asked this promise
  of me.
Finally I understood. It was not to make me grieve,
  but to make me think of the Lord
  whom my mother loved.
It was to make me want to love Him too.

A MOANING
IN THE MUSIC

1

It is August of 1850. I am now thirteen years old,
   standing in front of the mirror while my older sister
   Ellen brushes my hair.
"You have such beautiful golden hair, Fanny.
I shall miss brushing it for you."

I sigh and lean my elbows on the dressing table.
Sweet Nellie. Always mothering me, but somehow I
   don't mind.
"Nellie, it's not as if I'll be gone forever."

Ellen coils a strand of my hair around her finger.
She lets it go, and the ringlet bounces against
   my shoulder.
"Are you excited, Fanny? Going away to school
   will be one of the greatest events in your life."

I don't want my sister to know how jittery I feel inside,
   just like all the butterflies I've ever caught
   are trapped in me, doing a fluttery dance.
I try to answer in an airy, careless voice.
"I suppose I'm excited. It will be different
   from learning at home,

but I think I'll make new friends,
ever so many more than I've had before."
At least I hope so.
I fidget with one of the tassels on the lampshade.

Ellen is silent for a moment.
She leans over my shoulder.
We watch our faces together in the mirror.
"Oh, Fanny, think how greatly God loves you," she says.
"Mamma was always concerned for you, feared that you
    had never learned to love Him too. Now that you're
    going away . . ."

I stand up quickly from the dressing table.
I turn from the mirror before Ellen can see
    the guilty look,
    like a cloud crossing my face before a storm.
"I can't love God yet," I tell her.
I hurry from the room before she can answer,
    leaving her standing with the brush still in her hand.

2

The next day, I kiss my father goodbye
    and smile up at him.
"I shall miss you, Papa."

"You look so grown up, my dear."
Father helps me into the carriage and hands my trunk
    to the driver.
He leans in the window, that teasing look in his eyes.
"I should have hardly recognized my little songbird
    who loved to sit up in the trees and sing.
Study hard, Fanny, and do your best. God has given you

many gifts.
You will be able to develop them as never before."

Since Father cannot go with me, Maria is
    my traveling companion.
She will see me safely to the school in Belmont.
As I sit next to Maria in the carriage, I notice
    her calmness and poise.
I look down. I can see my own hands trembling
    in my lap,
        even inside my new white gloves.
I raise one shaking hand and wave to Papa
    as the carriage drives away.

The sun is setting when at last Maria and I enter the
    drawing room.
So this is Mrs. Teed's boarding school. I stretch
    my legs and arms,
        stiff from the jolting carriage ride, and look around.
All is tidy and well cared for.
A pleasant woman takes my hand.
Her eyes are warm and comforting,
    like a cup of tea at bedtime.
"So pleased to meet you, Frances," says Mrs. Teed.
"You and your sister may enjoy some refreshment alone.
Then I'll bring you in for prayer time."

The butterflies are dancing inside me again.
My hands rattle the china cup in its saucer.
I can eat only one small currant scone.
From another room I can hear voices of girls singing.

"That must be the schoolroom, Fanny," says Maria.
"How sweetly they sing that hymn.
It was one of Mamma's favorites."
Softly we move behind the door where we can listen.

I think that I have never heard anything so lovely.
The final notes die away, and Mrs. Teed steps out
   into the hall.
"Come inside," she says, smiling, reaching for my hand.
"You're just in time for the chaplain's address."

My eyes must be as wide as my china saucer at tea.
When I step through the doorway,
   I see a room full of young girls sitting quietly.
Never have I seen so many girls in one place before.
So many new friends to meet.

Mrs. Teed guides me to a seat in one of the empty desks.
As Reverend Parker speaks, all the excitement and strain
   of the day
   catch up with me, and my eyelids hang heavy.
I must not be so rude as to fall asleep.
I fight to stay awake.

But later I remember only a few things
Reverend Parker said in his short sermon.
"Begin your school term with the Savior.
Christ loved you and gave His life for you.
Live in a spirit of love toward one another."

That night I kneel beside my small white bed.
"Please help me, Lord.
I do want to begin to know You here at this school."

3

I enjoyed my life at Mrs. Teed's school. Very much.
I quickly lost my homesickness.
All the new experiences captured my full attention;

I had always loved learning.
My teachers knew their subjects well.
Music and art were my favorites.
And I discovered that I was good at languages.
French and Italian suited my tongue
    as if I were born into a band of roving minstrels.

Wouldn't Flo have loved to hear me conjugate the verb
    "to hunt" in French?

Je chasse le petit chien.
Tu chasses le petit chien.
Il chasse le petit chien.
Nous chassons le petit chien.
Vous chassez le petit chien.
Ils chassent le petit chien.

Truly, sometimes the whole family went *en poursuite*
    when Flo ran away.

We all spoke French to one another, even outside
    of classes.
Mrs. Teed required it.
I felt as if I spent the first month saying,
    "*Je m'appelle Frances. Et toi? Comment tu t'appelles?*"

For the first time in my life, I met many other girls
    my age.
Mary and Elizabeth were my closest friends.
I also admired Diana.
The truth is, I wanted desperately to be like Diana.
She was charming and kind, always.
I thought she must love God more than anyone else
    I knew.
I thought of her as the sunbeam of the school.

I soon discovered that Mrs. Teed cared about more
    than our schoolwork and our proper manners.
She cared about our souls.
Bible reading and prayer were part of our
    regular routine.
So was memorization.
What large portions of Scripture she required us
    to learn!
Some of the teachers had weekly prayer meetings
    for the girls in their rooms.
And often Mrs. Teed sought us out,
    one at a time, apart from the others,
    to speak to us alone about our relationship with Jesus.

I loved Mrs. Teed, and I wanted her to be pleased
    with me.
But I felt confused about my own heart.
Where did I stand with God?
I wanted to hide my doubts and questions
    from everyone around me.
During the day when my mind was busy
    with my music and my French,
    I could pretend that all was well.
But many nights I lay awake,
    staring wide-eyed at the moon
    through the curtainless windows.
Over and over again, I tried to pray.
I tried to feel love for God.
I wanted to be saved, but my heart was dark and joyless.
When would God take away the cloud of doubt,
    give me the peace and joy a Christian was supposed
    to have?
Perhaps I was like Flo.
Perhaps God was chasing me,
    but I was not quite ready to be caught.

Deep inside my heart,
  I was still running away.

4

Mary and I are walking in the school gardens
  during recess.
I take a deep breath. It is time; I must ask
  my burning question.
"Mary, do you love God?"

Mary glances over at me in surprise. "Of course I do.
I love Him more than I can tell vou."

Her prompt reply is like a stab in my heart.
If only I could feel the same confidence.
I put my face in my hands, and suddenly sobs shake
   my whole frame.

I feel Mary lay a hand softly on my shoulder.
"Frances? What's the matter?"

"I wish I could say that I love Him too," I tell her
   between sobs.
"I want to love Him, but I'm not able to."

Mary is quiet for so long that I begin to feel calm.
My breathing stills like the gentle rhythm of sea waves
   after a sudden squall. I finally lift my face to look
   at Mary.
Is she too shocked to answer me?

But no, Mary is watching me with kindness in her eyes.
I sniffle and take one more shaky breath.

"Frances," says Mary, "would you say that you are still
   a little child?"

I frown at this unexpected question.
I am thirteen,
   not exactly a *little* child, but not a grown woman either.
"I would say that I'm still a child."

"Well, then, listen to the Scripture we learned only day
   before last.
Jesus said, 'Suffer the little children to come unto me,
   and forbid them not.'
Remember how He took the little children
   into His arms?
You may go to Jesus like a little child.

Tell Him you want to love Him but cannot.
Ask Him to teach you."

I watch the shadows on the lawn
  as the sun moves out from behind the clouds.
I feel as though, just for a moment,
  the sun's light has shined into my heart.
Mary's words are so simple.
Could coming to Jesus be as simple as that?
Perhaps He is as kind and ready to help me as Mary is.
I wipe away the last of my tears and smile at my friend.

5

The end of the term was approaching.
I began to think about how long I had been away
  from home.
I had been so busy, I had hardly had time to miss
  my family.
But now I could not wait to see them.

I was seated across from Diana at tea one evening.
As usual I watched her face keenly.
Something was different about Diana.
I had seen her sitting by herself only the day before,
  looking as different from a sunbeam
  as winter from spring.
But tonight she was almost glowing.
Her eyes sparkled, her smile flashed often,
  her laughter bubbled up freely.
Perhaps, like me, she was merely excited to see her family.
But no, it was more than that.
It was like a burden had dropped from her shoulders.

When most of the girls had left the table,
  I leaned forward and whispered to her.
"Diana, what has happened to you?
For the last few days I have worried about you.
I thought your feelings were hurt about something.
But now you seem happier than ever."

To my surprise, Diana jumped out of her chair,
  came around to my side of the table,
  and threw her arm around me.
The sunbeam was certainly back,
  and shining brighter than ever.
"Oh, Fanny, I'm so happy!" she sang in my ear.
"Jesus has forgiven me at last.
Now I know He's my Savior."

I felt my jaw drop.
Diana? Forgiven? But she had been a Christian
  all along.
She must have been.
"Diana, you have been the best Christian at this school,
  this whole term!" I burst out.
"Always kind. Always cheerful.
Always surrounded by friends.
I've often thought if only I could become a Christian
  like you,
    I'd be happy."

Diana shook her head.
"It only seemed like that, Fanny, on the outside.
I knew how to act.
I knew the right things to say.
But I was proud.
On the inside I didn't want to admit
  that I had sins to be forgiven.
I started praying and seeking God in secret.

A few days ago I came across Jesus' words in my Bible:
  'Thy sins be forgiven thee.'
That's when it hit me.
I had never asked Jesus to forgive *my* sins.
And when I did, I found out how loving He is.
I hope you'll come to Him too, Fanny."

I left school at the end of the term with much
  to think about.
All three of my closest friends,
  Mary, Elizabeth, and Diana,
  had found peace with God at school.
I envied them. But I still could not find that same peace
  for myself.

6

In the hymns I wrote later,
  I never liked to dwell much
  upon these deep spiritual struggles of my youth.
But here I share a few lines from a poem I wrote in 1878,
  "The Key Found."
Early in the poem I wrote of the sorrow I felt
  during my long childhood season of doubt.
I thought about the way I often kept the sorrow
  locked inside me where no one could see it.
I remembered the tears that soaked my pillow
  during long, wakeful nights at Mrs. Teed's.

> *There is a strange wild wail around, a wail*
>   *of wild unrest,*
> *A moaning in the music, with echoes*
>   *unconfessed, . . .*

And deep, low, shuddering groans that rise
from caves of gloom within.

And then I thought about how Christ's salvation is
   like a key,
   touching all those hidden places of the soul,
   releasing all the mechanisms that unlock a heart.
My poem continues on a note of hope:

As the key is to the lock, when it enters quick
   and true,
Fitting all the complex wards that are hidden
   from the view,
Moving all the secret springs that no other finds
   or moves,
So is Jesus to the soul, when His saving power
   He proves.

This key was soon to fit into the lock
   of my sorrowing young soul.

PEACE IS MADE

1

I did not know when I left Mrs. Teed's school
   that I would never return.

Shortly after the school term ended,
   Mrs. Teed's boarding school had to close.
From my days at the school I carried away
   new knowledge, new friends,
   and a lifelong correspondent and kindred spirit,
   Elizabeth Clay.

I also carried away my persistent doubts
   about my standing with God.
At home for a few months, I struggled privately
   to find the same assurance my friends spoke of.
These months seem to me, looking back,
   as one long, bleak winter day.
Cold mists of doubt,
   chilly storms of temptation and inward strife,
   dim twilight of miserable and disappointed longing.
A few times I caught gleams of hope from God's Word.
But more often I found no light at all.
I stumbled about on the edge of a deep valley of despair.

Papa packed me off to Oakhampton to visit Miriam,
  my oldest married sister. No doubt
  he thought I needed cheering up.
Miriam and Henry Crane lived back in the Astley parish
  where I had been born.
How I loved their home.
I could never get my fill of
  the beauty of the hills
  and the joy of being with my sister's dear family.
This visit was to mark an important turning point
  in my young life.

2

"Fanny, you are up to your old tricks,
  leaving books of poetry about for people
  to stumble over."
Miriam smiles as she hands me the book I left lying
  on the parlor rug.
"I thought by the time you were fifteen
  you would have learned to pick up after yourself."

"At least I'm not reading in the hayloft anymore,"
  I point out.
"You have to admit I've grown a little more ladylike
  after my months at Mrs. Teed's."

Miriam tips her head, appraising me.
"A little," she says. "I will make that small concession.
Fanny, who do you think is coming to stay at
  Oakhampton for a week?"

"I cannot guess."

"Caroline Cooke. You remember her.
She was an old chum from my younger days."

"Oh, yes, Miss Cooke. Papa mentioned her recently.
Was she here during one of his visits?"

"Indeed, she was. I'll tell you a secret later.
But for now, help me put out fresh linens for her
    in the guest room."

Miss Cooke arrives in time for tea.
The next few hours are bright with happy conversation.

Then Miriam and her husband go upstairs to put
   their children to bed.
I find myself alone with Miss Cooke
   on the drawing room sofa.

"Won't you play something for me on the piano, Frances?
I've heard you're quite accomplished."

I stand and smooth my skirt. "Perhaps my sister
   has too high an opinion of my abilities.
But I'll be happy to play for you. Would you like
   a hymn?"

"I would indeed.
Could you play 'O God, Our Help in Ages Past'?"

I play and sing the familiar words of Isaac Watts,
and the sadness in my heart
wells up and floats on the surface.

> *O God, our help in ages past,*
> *Our hope for years to come,*
> *Our shelter from the stormy blast,*
> *And our eternal home!*

Slowly I lift my hands from the keys,
   and fold them in my lap. I feel my shoulders slump.
I feel Miss Cooke watching me.
When I move back to my seat,
   I see that her eyes are soft and kind.

"Is something wrong, Fanny?"

Tears spring to my eyes.
Before I can blink them away, one spills down my cheek.
I shrug. What does it matter if Miss Cooke knows
   about my struggles?
I have already told some of the girls at school.

I might as well tell this kind older woman
   who reminds me of Mamma in some ways.
Perhaps she can help.

"That hymn," I begin. "I'm not sure I believe it."

I glance up at Miss Cooke.
She shows no surprise. Her eyes are fixed on me steadily.
I swallow and plunge on.
"I've had a storm in my heart for so long now.
I can't seem to find any shelter in God.
I can't find much hope in His Word at all.
I don't know if I belong to Him.
I'm not sure I love Him enough to go
   to His eternal home.
I wish . . . I wish I knew that I were forgiven."
I hope Miss Cooke will not think me rude
   for blurting out something so personal.

More tears fall silently.
Miss Cooke hands me a pretty handkerchief trimmed
   in lace.
I blot my face with it and draw a shaky breath.
Somehow it feels good to cry.
The burden loses some of its weight, just by speaking
   of it.

"Fanny," asks Miss Cooke after a moment,
   "do you want to be forgiven?"

I nod vigorously. "Oh, yes!
It's more important to me than everything—
   more important than Papa and all my brothers
   and sisters.
I would give them all up
   if only I could know for sure that I was God's child."

Miss Cooke reaches out, touches my arm.
"Then Fanny, I am sure it will not be very long
   before your desire is granted."

The words are like a beautiful flower
   opening before my eyes.
I look up hopefully. "Do you really think so?"

Miss Cooke squeezes my arm gently.
"Fanny, why can you not trust yourself to the Savior
   at once?
Suppose Christ were to come right now
   in the clouds of heaven.
Suppose He were to call for all His redeemed ones.
Couldn't you trust Him then?
Wouldn't His promise be enough for you?
Couldn't you commit your soul to Him,
   to your Savior, Jesus?"

Stillness floods the room. I hold my breath.
The same thought from months before returns,
   flits across my mind again like a stray sunbeam.
Perhaps it is just that simple.
I have been striving, trying so hard to gain assurance.
But Jesus is only asking me to rest, to trust Him,
   to cease from my own efforts completely.
He has already paid the full price of my redemption
   with His blood.

Although twilight has dimmed the windows,
   the room seems to grow suddenly brighter.

I jump up. "Yes! Yes, I can trust Him.
Oh, Miss Cooke, you're right. Thank you, thank you!"

I run upstairs, taking the steps two at a time,
   slip into my room and shut the door.

I throw myself down on the little rug by the bed
　　and pour out my heart to the Lord.
With solemn joy and some lingering fear,
　　I commit my soul to Him.

And peace comes at last.

3

I often thought back to that moment.
I could never put an exact time on my first coming
　　to the Savior.

It seemed as if I had been trying to come for many years,
   moving forward a few steps,
   then backing away in fear and doubt.
But I know with complete certainty
   that I *did* trust the Lord Jesus that night.
Earth and heaven seemed bright from that moment.

The next few days were the happiest I had ever known.
For the first time in my life, the Bible seemed sweet
   to me.
I was hungry for its words,
   and I carried a New Testament in my pocket
   so I could sneak a few moments to read it
   whenever possible.
I pulled it out as I rode alone
   on the outside seat of the carriage on a family outing.
My eager fingers turned the pages to John 14,
   and I read aloud the words of Jesus.

"Let not your heart be troubled:
   ye believe in God, believe also in me.
In my Father's house are many mansions:
   if it were not so, I would have told you.
I go to prepare a place for you.
And if I go and prepare a place for you,
   I will come again, and receive you unto myself;
   that where I am, there ye may be also."

I turned my face into the wind, looked up at the sky.
At last I understood what Mamma meant
   on that long-ago day.
Pray to God to prepare you
   for all that He is preparing for you.
At last I could be sure.

God was preparing a place for me too,
    but I could be received there
    only through faith in Jesus Christ.
Now at last I was prepared.
A smile spread over my face.
"Thank you, Jesus," I whispered. "I believe."

4

I soon found out my sister's secret about Miss Cooke.
It was too wonderful!
Caroline Cooke and my father were engaged
    to be married.
I was so happy I felt I would burst.

The wedding took place that July.
I could not imagine a stepmother I could love
    more dearly
    than the woman who had helped me in my quest
    to belong to Christ.

I realized something else.
My new joy in Christ was an answer to the prayers
    of my own beloved mother.
Never had I forgotten Mamma's words
    from her sickbed.
"Remember, Fanny, nothing
    but the precious blood of Christ
    can make you clean and lovely in God's sight."

More than twenty years later,
    I penned the words to the hymn "The Precious Blood
    of Jesus."

Perhaps by writing the hymn, I could make certain
that the whole world remembered too.

Precious, precious blood of Jesus,
Shed on Calvary;
Shed for rebels, shed for sinners,
Shed for me.

Precious blood that hath redeemed us!
All the price is paid;
Perfect pardon now is offered,
Peace is made.

Precious, precious blood of Jesus,
Let it make thee whole;
Let it flow in mighty cleansing,
O'er thy soul.

Though thy sins are red like crimson,
Deep in scarlet glow,
Jesus' precious blood can make them
White as snow.

TRUEHEARTED, WHOLEHEARTED

1

It is August of 1851. And to my great joy,
  I am starting another year of school, this time
  nearer home.
Upon my arrival, I throw my arms around
  the headmistress.
"I'm so delighted to come to school, Miss Haynes!"

Miss Haynes's eyebrows shoot up,
  but she places her hands on my shoulders and smiles.
"We're delighted you're here, Frances.
I hope you will apply yourself to your studies."

"Yes, Miss Haynes, I promise I will."

And I do. I drink in everything I read in my books,
  everything I hear in my classes.
Long into the evenings, my study lamp burns.
And I rise early in the mornings
  to read my Bible and prepare for the new school day.

I have never been so busy,
  but I feel that I have never been happier.

One December morning, I awake hot and flushed,
   burning up with fever. When I look in the mirror,
   I see that an ugly rash has broken out over my face.
Miss Haynes summons a doctor.
Together they stand beside my bed,
   and their faces look grave.

"Erysipelas," says the doctor. "She must be sent home
   at once."

"Oh, dear." I hear Miss Haynes's voice as if
   from a great distance,
   but she sounds sad. "Frances loves school,
   and she has been working very hard at her studies.
She will be so disappointed."

"Nevertheless, she must go home." The doctor's voice
   is firm.
"The disease is extremely serious.
She must keep to her bed.
Without complete rest, she could go blind
   or even die."

Go blind. Or even die.
I try to process the words, but my brain feels fuzzy
   and the words make little sense.
"Could I please . . . have . . . some water?" is all
   I manage to say.

Back home in the St. Nicholas rectory, I lie in bed
   for many weeks.
Much of the time, I am too weak and tired even to read.
Sometimes Maria sits beside my bed and reads aloud.
But I am not permitted to do any studying
   or school work.

Papa often stands over me. Sometimes he touches
   my forehead
   with a sympathetic frown.
"You've always been my Little Quicksilver, Fanny.
So full of energy, so light on your feet.
To lie here so still must be a great trial."

Dear Papa.

2

By the end of the following summer,
   I was finally beginning to regain my strength.
But Papa was not well.
Ever since an accident in his carriage long ago,
   he had suffered from eye problems.
He now needed rest,
   so the whole family traveled to North Wales.

I sat beside Colwyn Bay, watching the gulls fly over
   the blue, blue sea.
I wrote to my friend Elizabeth,
   sneaking in a few Welsh words here and there,
   telling her my exciting news:
   I was growing stronger day by day,
   and I was learning to speak and read in Welsh.
But I also confided my sadness.

I wish I were not so impatient as I am
   at hearing the (to me) dreadful news
   that I must on no account go to school again
   till after Christmas, and perhaps not at all.
Oh, I am so disappointed.

I cannot bear to be ignorant and behind the others
in learning.

I paused for long moments, my pen poised to write,
    my heart remembering Job in the Bible.
He, too, had many disappointments
    and much greater suffering than mine.
Yet he trusted his heavenly Father,
    prepared to receive even death at His good hands.
When my pen touched the paper again,
    thoughts like those of Job spilled out in ink
    on the page.

If I receive good things at the hand of such a Father,
shall I murmur at this drawback?

At that time I did not know
    that I would never really be strong again.
For the rest of my life I went through seasons of illness,
    forced inactivity, long bedridden recoveries.
But the Bible I was learning to love
    would prove to be my lamp,
    its light pooling around me in those dark times.

3

Later that year Papa went to consult an eye doctor
    in Germany.
Mama (for that is what I called Miss Cooke now)
    and I traveled along with him.
My heart ached with the beauty of the scenery,
    the buildings of Dusseldorf rising above the Rhine.

Here, Papa said, I would finally be able to go
    to school again.

In the autumn of 1852, I was one of 110 girls
    enrolled at the Louisenschule in Dusseldorf.
At this school I must read, write, and speak only
    in German.
I plunged into my studies, enjoying the challenge.
I was able to take a drawing class,
    and the city all around me offered art—
    crumbling old castles,
    soaring cathedral spires,
    boats sailing on the river.

But perhaps my greatest challenge was my music lessons.
My teacher encouraged me to learn music
    by German composers.
He much preferred Mendelssohn to my "splashy
    English pieces."
And so I learned to love the German music too.

My letters to Elizabeth throughout these months
   were breezy and happy,
   but they did not tell the whole story.
I had my share of struggles at school too.
   Nearly every day I battled loneliness.
   Not one other girl of my acquaintance shared my faith.

4

I open my Bible,
   draw a sheet of paper from the writing desk,
   and pick up my pen. I write my heading with a flourish:
   My thoughts on Ephesians 4.

A sudden titter behind me makes me whirl around.
I am just in time to see the hems of two skirts
   disappear around the corner. I listen.
The girls' voices echo down the corridor as they
   hurry away.

"The *Englanderin* [English girl] is reading
   her Bible again.
If that were all I had to do for fun, I would go mad."

More laughter, and the other girl answers.

"My father says the Bible is just a crutch
   for people who do not want to think for themselves.
He says faith is for the weak-minded."

Their voices fade as they run lightly down the stairway.
I sigh and bow my head.

"Dear Lord, I don't think there is another girl here
   who cares for Your truth," I whisper.

"Please help me to walk worthy of my calling,
    as it says here in Ephesians.
Give me a stronger desire to witness for You.
Please let me win others to you.
And even when they are unkind, Lord,
    please keep my tongue from the unkind words I want
    to say back.
Please don't let me dishonor You."

5

Till that year at Louisenschule, I had spent all my life
    among Christians.
Never had I been in a place where so many opposed
    my beliefs,
    where so many were hostile and even rude.
We were not as strictly supervised
    as we would have been in an English school.
Hurtful teasing and cruel comments
    went without rebuke or punishment.
Sometimes I was tempted to hide my faith away inside.
Maybe if I didn't talk about Christ
    or read my Bible openly,
    the other girls would let me be.

Often I pictured myself sailing a ship all alone
    like the ones I saw on the Rhine,
    their battle flags flying high in the sun.
I had to come out more boldly on the Lord's side,
    raise His flag higher
    than I had ever done before.
The pressure was good for me;
    I grew in my faith.

And as the term went on,
   I began to see a change in some of the girls.
I tried to return kindness for their insults,
   and they found less and less enjoyment in making fun
   of me.
Though I did not know of any girls who came to Christ,
   some of them stopped teasing me,
   and a few even treated me with affection.

6

Dear Elizabeth,
You will like to know the result
   of my last examination.
Imagine my surprise when,
   with heart pounding and cheek burning,
I heard my name:
   "Frances Havergal, Numero Eins!"
You understand German enough to know
   that eins *means* one.
Me, a daughter of Britain.
I lay awake till nearly midnight
   for pure delight and satisfaction.

7

It was 1853, and I was now sixteen years old.
When I left the Louisenschule,
   I was a little sad to realize
   that I was leaving school behind forever.

From now on I would have to learn on my own.
Equally sobering was the knowledge that
   my childhood was over.
I must take the responsibilities of an adult,
   not the least of those being my own spiritual growth.
The rougher cutting of my spirit had been done
   by other hands.
Now, if it would ever be a diamond,
   I must polish and grind it myself
   with the help of the great Master Jeweler.

To my great delight, I was able to continue
   learning privately.
Since his eyes were not improving,
   Papa sought further treatment in Heidelberg.
He and Mama arranged for me to stay in the home of
   one of his fellow pastors in Obercassel.
Pastor Schulze-Berge and his wife welcomed me
   with open arms.
The shelves of their home were lined with books
   in both German and French.
They told me I might read to my heart's content.
For four hours every morning
   I studied German and French literature and history.
I especially admired the German poet Goethe.
Pastor Schulze-Berge discussed Goethe's works with me
   and helped me understand them.
Then I wrote my own compositions in German
   and gave them to the pastor for his criticism.

One day Pastor Schulze-Berge laid aside his copy
   of Goethe's *Faust* and said,
   "Frances, you have a rare talent for one so young.

It would take most German ladies years of study
to reach your level of understanding.
Your progress can only be called extraordinary."

But life was not all study and books.
I found time for rowing on the Rhine with the family,
and I even learned to handle the oars myself.
I befriended an aristocratic family nearby
and often received invitations for tea.
I wished that their relative,
an honest-to-goodness princess
would come and visit while I was there.
I had never spoken to a princess in my life.

8

Although I was young,
in those years I was making decisions
that would determine the course of my life.
Already I had learned that the Christian life
is more than joy, peace, and happy service.
I had experienced battle,
spiritual warfare both outward and inward.
And I believe even then I had determined
whose side I would be on, then and always.
Twenty years later, I wrote a hymn
expressing this early commitment to the cause of Christ.

> *True-hearted, whole-hearted, faithful and loyal,*
> *King of our lives, by Thy grace we will be!*
> *Under Thy standard, exalted and royal,*
> *Strong in Thy strength, we will battle for Thee.*

True-hearted, whole-hearted! Fullest allegiance
Yielding henceforth to our glorious King;
Valiant endeavor and loving obedience,
Freely and joyously now would we bring.

True-hearted! Saviour, Thou knowest our story;
Weak are the hearts that we lay at Thy feet,
Sinful and treacherous! yet, for Thy glory,
Heal them, and cleanse them from sin and deceit.

True-hearted, whole-hearted, Saviour all glorious!
Take Thy great power and reign there alone,
Over our wills and affections victorious,
Freely surrendered and wholly Thine own.

9

It is 1854. I am back in England,
　and it is July 17, my confirmation day.
I have looked forward to this day
　as long as I can remember.
In the Church of England, children
　are baptized as infants
　and only later in life
　do we make a public commitment to follow Christ.
I desperately wanted my confirmation
　to be more than just words,
　to be more than an effort to please my parents,
　but to come from the depths of my heart.

This morning I am up before the sun,
　kneeling beside my bed,
　trying to pray. I am distracted.
I think back on all the doubts,

all the struggles and trials
of my faith during my young life.
But there have been victories too.

"Thank you, Jesus.
I praise You for bringing me all the way
to this day, weak and sinful though I am."

I walk to the Worcester Cathedral
in a procession with the other candidates.
With each step my heart pounds.
The weight of what I am about to do
lies heavy upon me.
I remember the words of Scripture:
"Now unto him that is able to keep you from falling,"
and I am comforted.

When the bishop lays his hands on me,
I follow his prayer in my heart,
thrilling with longing and joy at the words
"Thine for ever."

10

I jotted a short poem that formed in my mind
during the service in the cathedral.

"Thine For Ever"

*Oh! "Thine for ever," what a blessed thing
To be for ever His who died for me!
My Saviour, all my life Thy praise I'll sing,
Nor cease my song throughout eternity.*

I never got over the thrill
  of this solemn commitment to Christ.
Every year afterwards on July 17
  I celebrated the anniversary of that day.

TENDER LAMBS

1

I pressed on in my private studies,
  reading German, French, and English.
With my father's help I began to learn Greek.
What a whole new world of enjoyment
  this opened up to me.
Now I could study the New Testament
  in its original language.

And I wrote poems, sometimes just for fun.
I wrote verses for my nieces and nephews
  in honor of their birthdays.
I loved them as if they were my own children,
  and I longed for them to live for God.
I wrote these lines for my nephew
  John Henry Crane on his third birthday:

> *Love is watching round thee now,*
> *Tracing sunbeams on thy brow;*
> *Never be her mission done*
> *To thy father's only son!*

Yet a higher, deeper love
Watcheth o'er thee from above
Then thy fount of motive be
Love to Him who loveth thee.

I also began publishing some of my poems and riddles
   in the magazines and short collections of verse
   so popular in my Victorian times.
I wrote under a pen name to protect my privacy.

2

"What do you think of this one, Maria?"
I push a sheet of paper in front of my sister
   as she sits reading by the fire.
I pull up a footstool and perch on it.
"Do you think people will be able to solve this riddle?
Tell me if it's too hard."

Maria's lips move quietly as she reads over the lines.
She thinks for a moment,
   looks up at me,
   smiles.
"Is it one word?"

I nod eagerly.

"I will try to solve it," says Maria.
"I shall read it aloud."

   Arise, my first! In peerless radiance beaming,
   A veil of glory thou dost weave for earth:
   The ocean waves to welcome thee are gleaming,
   For thou alone to Beauty givest birth.

"Hmmmm.
I think that is describing the sun.
It certainly is radiant,
   and we couldn't see any of earth's beauty without it."

I grin. "You are right.
The first syllable of the word is *sun*."

She pencils *sun* next to the lines and reads on.

> *Shine forth, my second! Freshly now is flowing*
> *The busy stream of life, and labor too;*
> *Each heart with ardor, base or noble glowing,*
> *Till thou shalt close, arresting all they do.*

"I think that verse describes *day*.
People do their work during the day,
   and they have to stop at its close."

"Right again." I watch her pencil in the word *day*.

"And now the next verse must be putting them
   together—*Sunday*."

> *All hail, my whole! thou comest with rich pleasure*
> *An angel from the land of pure delight,*
> *The great man's blessing, and the poor man's*
> *   treasure,*
> *Our earnest of the day which knows no night.*

Maria's eyes sparkle.
"Ah, yes. Sunday, the great man's blessing
   and the poor man's treasure,
   and, indeed, a little foretaste of heaven.
A fitting description of the Lord's Day.
Good work, Frances.
It will make a more thought-provoking riddle
   than the common ones tossed about in parlor games."

3

I never kept the money
    I received in payment for my poems.
I decided that the money would belong to the Lord.
I gave it to the Church Missionary Society
    and other charities.

Papa was now back in his pulpit,
    and I taught in the children's Sunday school.
I loved "my children" with an intensity
    that drove me to my knees for them.
Night after night I prayed
    for each child in the class.
The disobedient ones I wept over.
I often visited their homes,
    urging them to make sure of their salvation.
I later learned that one of my most troublesome boys
    had become an ordained minister.

That year I visited my sister Nellie,
  wife of Giles Shaw, in Ireland.
She invited schoolgirls to take singing lessons from me.
I made a special friend, a little invalid girl
  who had to stay in bed.
My own battle with erysipelas
  was still a vivid memory,
  and I knew how she felt.
I visited as often as I could,
  read God's Word with her,
  taught her some Greek and even a bit of Hebrew.

Back at home again, my friend Elizabeth and I
  would often leave Worcester,
  going out to the countryside to walk.
We worked on Scripture memory
  just as we had done at Mrs. Teed's,
  quizzing ourselves with long passages,
  repeating alternate verses to each other,
  the Gospels, the Epistles, Revelation,
  Isaiah, and the Psalms.
I loved life; I was busy and happy,
  until one day . . .

4

"Fanny, sit down."

"What is it, Papa?"
I do not like the furrow between his brows.

"I have seen the doctor today.
And I have made a decision.

I must resign from my work
    at St. Nicholas Parish Church."

"Oh, Papa, where will we go?
What will you do?"

"I've been offered a living at Shareshill.
It is a small rural parish,
    quieter than this busy city work.
I wrote my letter of acceptance today.
I know you will be sorry to leave the children, Fanny.
I am sorry too."

5

"Look what just arrived."
I hold up a package.
"It's from the Sunday school children."

Maria looks up from the trunk
    where she and Mama are packing
    carefully wrapped dishes.
If I wrapped up my heart in paper,
    could I keep it from breaking?

There are books in the package.
I open the top one and read
    a child's note, scrawled on the flyleaf.
My eyes fill with tears.
"I will miss them so.
God knows how much I loved them
    and prayed for them.
Now I must ask Him to bring fruit from their lives
    even if I'm not here to see it."

6

My own special class gave me a pencil case,
   which I always treasured.
And one day I drew out a pencil and wrote
   this poem in memory of those dear ones.

> *O Thou who gatherest with loving arm*
> *The tender lambs, who in each dark alarm*
> *Wilt fold them safely,—listen to my prayer . . .*
> *O Saviour, . . . to these extend Thy love,*
> *And let them know its sweetness . . .*
> *May they reflect Thine image pure and bright*
> *As burnished silver, spotless in Thy sight;*
> *Cleansed by Thy blood from every sinful stain,*
> *Let not its stream pour for them in vain. . . .*
> *And in the Book of Life let each one be*
> *Inscribed as in eternal lines by Thee!*

7

Papa and I sit by the fire in our new home.
I can tell he has something to say,
   and yet he is quiet.
"What did you want to talk to me about, Papa?"

"Frances, my dear, I think you need
   a change of scene."
He jabs the poker into the fire.
Sparks shoot up. The fire leaps larger.
I watch it in silence, waiting.

"You've been studying so hard
  since coming here to the new parish.
I fear the long hours at the books are not kind to you.
Your health has always been delicate,
  yet you seem paler and quieter than usual.
Where is my Little Quicksilver?"

I chuckle at the old nickname.
Then I sigh.
"I just don't feel as useful here in Shareshill
  as I did in Worcester, Papa.
I miss my Sunday school children,
  my tender little lambs.
The people here are kind,
  but I have no class to teach.
And so I fill the hours with study.
I'm sorry, Papa. I shall try to spend more time
  taking walks in the village,
    enjoying the fresh air."

Papa pulls an envelope from his pocket.
"I have a proposal for you."

I lean forward,
    straining to see the handwriting on the letter.
"It's Miriam's hand. Is it from Oakhampton?"

"It is indeed."

"How are the children?
John Henry must be quite the little man.
And the girls, Miriam and Evelyn,
    are they getting along well in their studies?"

Papa puts on his glasses,
    clears his throat.
"It's interesting that you should ask," he says,
    "for that is exactly what your sister writes about.
How would you like to go there,
    not just for a visit,
    but to live for a few years
    and help with your nieces' lessons?
God has gifted you in learning, you know.
You would make an excellent teacher.
What do you say?"

I jump from my chair, bounce on my tiptoes.
"Oh, Papa!"

His eyes crinkle as he laughs.
"I shall take that as a yes."

"But you and Mama? I should be sorry to leave you.
I am needed to help care for you here."

Papa folds the letter, removes his glasses.
"Your mother and I are doing much better
    in this milder climate.

Maria will be here to help.
I think that God has stirred your heart to go,
  and go you must."

IN THY SERVICE GLAD AND FREE

1

And so I packed my bags.
I arrived at my sister's home in February of 1861.
Thus began my lovely years at Oakhampton
   as tutor to my nieces.

I may not have been the strictest disciplinarian,
   but I tried to make learning fun.
And we never lacked for recreation.
Riding, swimming, skating,
   croquet and chess,
   trips to the seaside and abroad.

Whenever I could,
   I squeezed in a little time for my own learning.
I continued my Latin,
   and I began Italian in earnest—the language
   of the great singers.
I also worked on my music.
I discovered that I loved writing my own songs.
And sometimes I was asked to perform
   at dinner parties, at community concerts.
Other people seemed to enjoy my music too.

"Oh Fanny, you should have heard
   the director of the Philharmonic
   praising your talent," Miriam told me once.

I sighed. "I love singing at the Philharmonic concerts.
And Dr. Marshall has been kind
   to give me singing lessons.
But I fear . . ."

"What do you fear, Frances?"

"I fear I love people's praise too much.
Maybe performing my music
   is puffing me up with pride."

Not long after this, I became ill,
   and for many weeks I could no longer sing
   at the concerts.
I remembered a prayer I had written.
"Oh that God would purify me . . . at any cost."

"God is purifying me now," I realized.
He cared too much to let me go on in my pride.
I thanked Him for protecting me
   from myself.

2

During this time of my life
   I had some proposals of marriage.
My desire to be a wife and mother
   wrung my heart.
How I loved children.
   And how I longed for a husband's love,
   protection, and close companionship.

But I knew I could marry
  only a believer in my Lord Jesus
  and only one who was
  truehearted, wholehearted.
And so I knew my answer to these offers
  must be no.

"Why aren't you married, Aunt Frances?"
  my curious nieces often asked
  as we talked in my room at night.
"Don't you feel lonely sometimes?
Don't you want a husband
  and children of your own?"

"Of course, I do, if God wills.
And in the meantime, I have you."

And then sometimes we would throw pillows
  and squeal with giggles
  until Miriam came to the doorway.
"To bed now, all of you," she would say,
  and put on a stern expression
  with a smile twitching behind it.

Of course, I knew the pain of loneliness.
And I knew that if my life was to be
  a lonely one,
  I must pray for the love of Jesus
  to be poured in
  and to satisfy my heart.
I could tell Him all about it,
  and Him alone.

3

In 1865 I returned to Germany
　just for a visit.
My friends the Schulze-Berges
　had a recommendation for me.
"We think you should visit the German composer
　Ferdinand Hiller
　to get his opinion on the musical works you
　have written."

Ferdinand Hiller,
　the foremost authority on music and composing
　in the world today.
At least in Pastor Schulze-Berge's opinion.

My answer was quick.
"Oh, I couldn't. I couldn't
　face his criticism.
He would just quench all the joy
　I find in writing my songs."

Mrs. Schulze-Berge watched me in her quiet way.
"You may as well know if the songs
　have promise, Fanny dear," she said.

And so I wrote to Dr. Hiller.
His reply was kind, and to my surprise,
　he set up an appointment to see me.

4

With sweaty palms, I knock at his door.
I am received into the very best kind of room,
  a room littered with books and sheets of music,
  and in the center, a handsome grand piano.
"Miss Havergal," says the elderly man politely,
  "I am glad you have come.
You have brought your work to show me?"

"Yes, sir." My voice is shaky,
  and I clear my throat nervously.

"Ah. I will look at it now.
Here is a book of poetry.
You may amuse yourself with it
    while I read through your manuscripts."

I can only pretend to read the poems.
Every few minutes I glance up at him,
    as he sits reading in silence.
I try to read his expression as his eyes scan
    page after page.

He looks up suddenly,
    fixes me with his piercing gaze.
"What instruction have you had?"

"I have a musical father, sir.
I go to him for help with the difficult parts."

"But what musical course have you gone through?
Who was your professor?"

I lower my eyes.
    "I've had no formal training in composing."

I feel my face reddening
    as Dr. Hiller stares at me.
I should never have come.

"I find that remarkable, Miss Havergal.
These songs bear the mark of talent.
Not genius, mind you, but talent.
Your melodies are pleasing, and some quite good.
However, your harmonies are astonishing."

"Thank you, sir."

"It is unusual, I must say,
  to find such a good grasp of harmony
  where there has been such limited training."

I lean forward, daring to look up at him again.
"Sir, you've been very generous and kind.
My question is not so much whether I have talent
  to write a few things for the pleasure
  of family and friends.
I am wondering whether my gifts are such
  that I could pursue music as my life's work."
I hold my breath, awaiting his answer.

Dr. Hiller closes my manuscript, removes his spectacles.
He looks at me with his keen eyes.
"Sincerely and unhesitatingly,
  I can say that you have such gifts."

I nearly float as I leave his studio.
I can hardly wait to tell Papa.

5

In 1866 my nieces went away for school.
I returned to my parents' home
  with a somewhat heavy heart.
What was next for me?

One afternoon I was cleaning a bureau drawer,
  and I found my diary.
I had kept the diary for several years,
  a little account of God's dealings with me,
  and a record of my spiritual progress.

I sat and read it straight through,
   while the shadows gradually lengthened
   with the setting sun.

What grace and mercy was mine!
Alas, no one professing to be a Christian
   could have had a more cloudy, fearing,
   doubting, sinning, and wandering heart history
   than mine through those many years.
And yet my God had brought me through
   my soul's darkest hours.
He had put gladness in my heart.

That day I wrote my last entry in the diary.
I would keep it no more.
My love for God was real; I knew that now.
By closing the book I made a decision
   to end my painful struggle with doubt at last.

I do love God.
I think I have loved Him more
   and longer than I thought,
   only I dared not own it to myself.
Oh that I loved Him more and more.

6

Around this time I penned the words to two poems
   addressed to "Jesus, Master."
The poems express my sense
   of indebtedness to Him.
Many hymnals have combined them into one hymn.

Jesus, Master, whose I am,
Purchased Thine alone to be,
By Thy blood, O spotless Lamb,
Shed so willingly for me;
Let my heart be all Thine own,
Let me live to Thee alone.

Jesus, Master! I am Thine;
Keep me faithful, keep me near;
Let Thy presence in me shine
All my homeward way to cheer.
Jesus! at Thy feet I fall,
Oh, be Thou my All-in-all.

Jesus, Master, whom I serve,
Though so feebly and so ill,
Strengthen hand and heart and nerve
All Thy bidding to fulfill;
Open Thou mine eyes to see
All the work Thou hast for me.

Jesus, Master! wilt Thou use
One who owes Thee more than all?
As Thou wilt! I would not choose,
Only let me hear Thy call.
Jesus! Let me always be
In Thy service glad and free.

DARKEST HOUR IS NEAREST DAWNING

1

My pen moves quickly across the crisp sheet of paper.

Dear Elizabeth,
My first note in my new room in our new home must be
to you.
It is solemn to think what I may go through in this room:
probably many happy hours, certainly many
sorrowful ones.

I pause to glance around at the thick carpets,
the rich, dark wood furnishings. I sigh.
The style of a table leg or the weave of a rug
is not important to me,
but my parents wanted well-appointed rooms.
I like having the room at the top of the house.
The quietest room in a home always suits my work
the best.
I continue my letter.

It will probably be my room until the great sorrow falls
which has often seemed as if it could come at any time,
unless I die before my precious father.

Our family's move to our new home in Leamington
    was once again for my father's health.
The town of Leamington was one of the earliest
    in England
    to have warm saltwater baths.
Visitors come from all over England
    to soak in the baths, and many have found relief from
    stiffness and pain.

But in spite of the health benefits of Leamington Spa,
    I know Papa is nearing the end of his life.
I cannot imagine life without him.
Our walks in the garden,
    his answers to all my most difficult questions,
    his help with my music,
    his thoughtful criticism of my poems,
    his strong voice swelling through the drawing room
    as I accompany his singing . . .
    these are things I love,
    and things I fear to lose.

2

The first great sorrow that visited me in that room
    came as a sad surprise a few months later.
It was not the death of my father,
    but of my young niece and former pupil, Evelyn Crane.
I had led Evelyn to Christ three years before.

One evening shortly after Evelyn's death,
    I sat curled up in a chair by the fire with a little packet
    from Maria.
Maria was at Oakhampton helping Miriam go through

Evelyn's things
  and had sent me one of the young girl's possessions,
  her small gold ring.
Of all Evelyn's belongings, it is the one
  I would cherish the most.
It took me back to a warm midsummer night
  five years ago
  when I had been living in Miriam's home
  as tutor for my nieces.
Closing my eyes, I relived the memory.

3

Evelyn stands at the open window in my room,
  looking out at the sunset.
I watch her with the special tenderness I feel
  for both girls.
They seem almost like my own daughters.
I know I need to send Evelyn off to bed,
  but I hate to put an end to our lively conversation
  about growing up.

Evelyn turns from the window suddenly,
  a teasing light in her big brown eyes.

"When I grow up, I'm going to be just like you,"
  she says.
She snatches my ring from the bedside table, puts it
  on her finger.
Then she twirls in her nightgown
  with her hand outstretched,
  watching the blue gems gleam.

"Look at my ring, my pretty ring!"
She jumps onto my bed, giggling. "It's mine now."

I turn my chair toward the bed.
Evelyn looks so lovely and graceful,
  laughing and tipping her wrist up and down
  so the ring will catch the light.

"Someday, you know," I tell her,
  "a long time from now, you might wear another ring
  on that left hand."

Evelyn's eyes sparkle. "Yes, I know. My wedding ring."
She looks down at the blue gemstones
  with the small diamond in the center.
"But I think I like your ring better than a wedding ring.
It has such pretty colors."

I smile at her. "Then it shall be yours someday.
But not today. It will be yours after I'm gone."

Evelyn's smile fades. She glances up quickly
  into my face.
"Gone? Where are you going?"

I stand up and walk over to the bed,
  sit down beside Evelyn, take the small ringed hand
  in my own.
"Darling, someday your Aunt Frances will die
  and go to be with Jesus in heaven.
Remember how we've talked about what happens
  after death?"

Evelyn stares at me.
She pulls away her hand, lifts the ring to her lips,
  kisses it fiercely. "Yes," she says.
"I will always wear it."

Then she quickly pulls it off her finger and hands it
  back to me.
She looks up with tears shining in her eyes.
"But no, Aunt Frances. I hope I shall never wear it.
I don't want you to die."

4

I open my eyes, coming back
  to the present and the light of the flickering fire.
I pick up the small gold band that Evelyn wore
  the last day I saw her,
  a beautiful young girl waving as she left for school.

Then I look at the blue gems sparkling on my own finger.
I never expected to be left with her ring instead
  of leaving her with mine.

"Someday I'll see her again," I whisper,
  "wearing a shining white robe and welcoming me
  in heaven.
But she got her wish. She will never wear my ring."
I kiss Evelyn's ring and slip it on my pinkie finger
  beside the blue-gemmed ring on my ring finger.
On the back of Maria's letter I scribble some lines
  of a new poem.

  Two rings are always on my hand,
  The azure and the gold,
  And they shall gleam together till
  My tale of life is told.

5

A year later in May,
  a special dream of mine came true.
Evelyn's parents invited me to go with them
  to Switzerland.
We traveled through the Alps.
I worked so hard to find the perfect words
  to describe the sight
  of a waterfall tumbling into a snowy stream.

Wild rapids, sheets of glass-like transparency,
  flowing swiftly . . . into emerald and snow. . .,
  shattered diamonds by millions leaping and glittering
  in the sunshine . . .
Every drop is so full of light that the eye is soon
  dazzled and weary.

One morning the sun rose above the mist.
From our window I could see
    the Bernese Oberland mountain peaks covered in snow.

So now the dream of all my life is realized;
    I have seen snow mountains!
I never saw anything . . . earthly . . .
    which so seemed to lead up to the unseen,
    to be the very steps of the Throne.

A dream come true, that trip.
And yet, in God's goodness to me,
    it was not to be the only one.
My travels were to bring me back to that beloved land
    again and again.
It was to become my place of rest and healing
    and, in a sense, my mission field.

6

Easter of 1870 was Papa's last Sunday.
He had felt well that morning and had gone for a walk.
Shortly afterward, he had a stroke,
    lost consciousness, and never awakened.
Two days later he was with his Lord.

For me, it was like night had fallen,
    and for a while I thought the sun would
    never rise again.

Dear Elizabeth,
I was terribly upset last night.
One of Papa's chants was gloriously sung
    at the evening service . . .

There are some sorrows that cannot be put into words,
and may only be wordlessly laid before God.

I put down my pen and walked to the window.
I could not let my sadness keep me from my work.
I must think about what the Lord wanted me to do next.
Perhaps organize a music class for children
    in Leamington.
Perhaps write music.

Suddenly I knew what to do.
Papa had wanted to prepare his psalm settings
    for publication.
He was never able to do it.
But I could.

I began work right away on putting the psalms to music.
Papa had already written many of his own tunes.
I was able to use my understanding of harmony
    to add beauty to those tunes.
I also composed some of my own.

7

"Mama, listen to me play this tune on the pianoforte."

I play the cheerful psalm tune with a lively flair.
Mama claps her hands.
"Oh, Fanny, how your father would have loved it."

I look over at my stepmother and smile.
"I was having so much trouble with it
    this morning, Mama.

I was puzzling over it for a long time,
  and I realized Papa
  would have decided about the tune in a minute.
That made me miss him.
But then this verse flashed into my mind:
  'Thou art the helper of the fatherless.'
And it was true. God helped me with it."

She smiles too, with tears behind the smile.
We both miss him.

8

Many of the psalm settings were later published
  in the hymnal I worked on with Mr. Charles Snepp,
  Songs of Grace and Glory.
Several of my original hymns were published as well,
  including "I Gave My Life for Thee."
That title had come to me
  from a caption beneath a picture of Jesus
  that I had seen in the study of Pastor Schulze-Berge.
After writing a few lines, I had decided to give up.
I threw my paper into the fire,
  but out it fell again, unharmed.
I took it up again and began afresh.
I wrote it as though Christ were speaking,
  gently reminding believers that they owed Him
  their lives and service.
Dear Papa had written a tune for it himself.

> *I gave My life for thee,*
> *My precious blood I shed,*
> *That thou might ransomed be,*

And quickened from the dead.
I gave My life for thee;
What hast thou given for me?

One gift I offered Him was my writing.
Writing was praying with me,
  and I prayed over every line, even over specific words.
It was shortly before Papa's death that my first book
  of poems,
  The Ministry of Song, was printed.
It is a special blessing that Papa knew of it,
  dear Papa who worked more than anyone
  to develop me as a musician and a writer.

9

I was learning that life is a mix of sorrow and joy.
The sorrow deepens us, makes us able
  to feel the pain of others.
And sorrow also taught me
  to dig deeply into God's Word for the comfort I needed.
How I loved the Bible.
Reading it helped me look forward to the day
  when my Savior would wipe away all tears
  from my eyes.

While on the trip to Switzerland,
  I had written a hymn called "Evening Tears and
  Morning Songs"
  after a long day of rain.
Looking out the hotel room window in the evening,
  I saw that the sky had turned bright
  and the clouds floated peacefully by.

I began writing a hymn text based on Psalm 30:5.

In the evening there is weeping,
Lengthening shadows, failing sight:
Silent darkness slowly creeping
Over all things dear and bright.

In the morning cometh singing,
Cometh joy and cometh sight,
When the sun ariseth, bringing
Healing on his wings of light.

Art thou weeping, sad and lonely,
Through the evening of thy days?
All thy sighing shall be only
Prelude of more perfect praise.

Darkest hour is nearest dawning,
Solemn herald of the day;
Singing cometh in the morning,
God shall wipe thy tears away!

SOME MOUNTAIN DAYS

1

In June of 1871 Elizabeth and I
traveled to Switzerland.
We carried only carpet bags for luggage,
and we had determined not to have a strict agenda.
We wanted to feel free to explore side roads
and stop to enjoy beautiful views.

We trekked the snow slopes overlooking the Furka Horn
and climbed the Eggishorn.
Glissading down was simply delicious.
Alpine dawn and sunset thrilled my heart
with their glorious color.

Hardly ever had I felt so wildly free and happy.
I hadn't thought I could feel this way again
after Papa died,
but I found healing in the bracing air,
the rushing streams,
the snow-capped peaks.
Truly in the morning joy does come.

The trip was not purely for tourism.
We also wished to be useful in the Lord's work.
We took along a collection of books and tracts in French
and were very pleased at their reception.
The people seemed delighted with them.
I spoke with one of our Alpine guides about reading
the Bible.
I prayed the Holy Spirit would become his Guide.

2

Even in Europe I found God giving me
the ministry of song,
opportunities to play and sing music for others.
One morning after breakfast in our hotel, Elizabeth and I
found a piano tucked away in the salon.
It was in tolerably good tune, and the first we'd had
on this journey.
I could not resist its call to me to sing and play;
And it seemed it would not create a disturbance,
There being only two other ladies in the room.

I played a bit, and then began to sing.
Imagine my surprise upon concluding my song
when the room behind me burst into loud applause.
Quietly behind my back, the room had filled
with Italians
who were urging me to continue.
I saw the waiter bringing more chairs,
and so of course I could not refuse their request.
I sang two more songs about my Lord.

3

In 1873 I returned to my beloved Switzerland
  in the company of the Snepp family
  whom I had helped with the hymnal.
What precious times I had with Mr. and Mrs. Snepp
  and their daughter Emily.
And yet I cannot forget the narrow escape we had.

We were coming down the snowy mountain roped together,
  first our guides, then me, then Mr. Snepp.
I was overconfident and thought it was safe
  to descend rather carelessly.
Suddenly I slipped, and the guide next to me
  lost his footing at the same time.

I was spinning down the steep incline,
   spinning too rapidly toward a sheer precipice,
   and I knew that the guides could not stop me.
In an instant, Mr. Snepp flung himself on his back,
   dug his heels into the snow,
   and with a snap, the rope went taut again.
We recovered ourselves.

Thank God for Mr. Snepp's quick thinking.
Sometimes my heart just craves speed,
   yearns for the sound of the wind rushing past
   as I slip and slide down the snowy slope.
But I must remember to listen to the guides
   when they caution me to go carefully.

4

I have discovered that a great deal of living
   must go into a very little writing.
So much of what God allows me to experience
   shows me deeper truths from His Word.
The beauty of the mountains reminds me
   that "the works of the Lord are great,
   sought out by all who have pleasure therein"
   (Psalm 111:2).

Just as the Alpine guides are there for my help and safety,
   I'm reminded that my Lord's words of caution
   are also for my safety and my good.
I must listen to my heavenly Guide as well.

And just as the Alpine ropes are run through
   with a red thread,
   a mark of strength and reliability,

the strong cord of God's eternal purpose and love
runs through my salvation,
unites me to Him in a bond that cannot be broken.

5

I had a walking stick, my staff,
    that I took with me on each trip,
    and I carved into it the names of mountain passes
    I reached in my climbs.
Eying the rough engravings on my staff one day,
    I wrote a sonnet.
Perhaps it is just as important, or even more so,
    to keep track of spiritual high points,
    those "red-letter days" on the calendar,
    in a similar way, for encouragement.

My Alpine staff recalls each shining height,
Each pass of grandeur with rejoicing gained,
Carved with a lengthening record, self-explained,
Of mountain-memories sublime and bright.
No valley-life but hath some mountain days,
Bright summits in the retrospective view,
And toil-worn passes to glad prospects new,
Fair sunlit memories of joy and praise.
Grave on thy heart each past 'red letter day!'
Forget not all the sunshine of the way
By which the Lord hath led thee: answered prayers
And joys unasked; strange blessings, lifted cares,
Grand promise-echoes! Thus thy life shall be
One record of His love and faithfulness to thee.

EVER, ONLY,
ALL FOR THEE

1

The year 1873 is drawing to a close.
I am visiting at Winterdyne, the English home
  of my sister Nellie,
    returned now from Ireland these seven years.
When the mail is placed in my hands this particular day,
  I receive a letter from a friend.
Inside is a little book entitled *All for Jesus*.

I do not know when I first open it
  and scan its contents
  that it will be life-changing.
The book speaks of consecration,
  of being set apart for Christ
  to a fuller degree than I have yet experienced.
I know I love Jesus; I have loved Him for a long time
  and often with a great intensity I can scarcely describe.
But this book speaks to me
  of coming nearer still,
  of knowing the power of His resurrection
  with the fellowship of His sufferings.

And it says this consecration is not only
    for my own blessing,
    but so that others will be blessed through me.

I have never believed we can reach sinless perfection;
    I know our struggles with the flesh make that impossible.
But I do want to be consecrated,
    to be "all for Jesus,"
    with a deep longing I have never felt before.
And I see that it is possible to make a fuller surrender,
    even long after a surrender
    has once or many times been made.

2

After my discovery that I needed to surrender my life
    more fully to Jesus,
I began to see constellations of promises
    shining in the Scriptures.

> *The blood of Jesus Christ, His Son,*
> *cleanseth us from all sin.*
>
> *Taking the shield of faith,*
> *wherewith ye shall be able to quench*
> *all the fiery darts of the wicked.*
>
> *God is able to make all grace abound toward you;*
> *that ye, always having all sufficiency in all things . . .*
>
> *My God shall supply all your need.*

I longed for others to taste this same goodness
    of the Lord.

3

It was shortly after this that my best-known hymn,
  known to many as the "Consecration Hymn,"
  had its birth.

I was visiting in a household of friends,
  a short visit of five days.
There were ten persons in the house,
  some unconverted,
  and some joyless Christians.
I prayed before the visit
  that God would give me an opportunity
  to speak of Him to all ten people in that home.

He granted my desire.
On the last night of my visit,
  I was so happy I could not sleep.
The couplets of the hymn
  chimed in my heart one after the other,
  and so I rose and wrote them down.

> *Take my life, and let it be*
> *Consecrated, Lord, to Thee.*
>
> *Take my moments and my days;*
> *Let them flow in ceaseless praise.*
>
> *Take my hands, and let them move*
> *At the impulse of Thy love.*
>
> *Take my feet and let them be*
> *Swift and 'beautiful' for Thee.*
>
> *Take my voice, and let me sing*
> *Always, only, for my King.*
>
> *Take my lips, and let them be*
> *Filled with messages for Thee.*

Take my silver and my gold;
Not a mite would I withhold.

Take my intellect and use
Every power as Thou shalt choose.

Take my will, and make it Thine;
It shall be no longer mine.

Take my heart, it is Thine own;
It shall be Thy royal throne.

Take my love; my Lord, I pour
At Thy feet its treasure-store.

Take myself, and I will be
Ever, only, all for Thee.

4

Something happened shortly after that night that gave
    me great joy.
I was at a large London party,
    and I was asked to sing.
Now I had a decision to make.
Would I keep my own commitment to sing
    "always, only, for my King"?

I decided to sing for Jesus,
    and I sang not only *for* Him but also *of* Him.
When I finished, I was met with dead silence.

But I was not discouraged.
Rather, I was happy that He had given me
    freedom and a sense of His presence while I sang.

After my singing, some of the party guests wanted
    to talk with me.
One was a complete stranger.
He began with a few witty remarks,
    but our talk quickly drifted to the subject of Christ.
He was interested and open,
    and he even thanked me at the end of it.

Let us sing words which we feel and love.
Let us look up to meet His smile while we sing.
Our songs will reach more hearts than those
    of finer voices.

5

It is January 1874.
The letter I just received sits open,
    its single page unfolded on my writing desk.
It is from my publisher in America.
I have been expecting the letter,
    but not this news contained in it.

I catch my breath, and read the words again.

*We regret to inform you that
    under the present circumstances,
    we will no longer be able to continue our operations.*

"Failed," I murmur.
"My American publisher has failed
    in the economic crisis.
And I have signed a contract with them.
I cannot seek publication with any other publisher
    in America."

This publisher had planned to publish two of my works,
  a children's story and a book of poems.
I bury my face in my hands
  and pause to consider all that this means.
I had hoped to hear news that my works
  were already disappearing off the booksellers' shelves
  faster than anyone expected.
This is what I dreamed of.
But I realize now that this is the end
  of my prospects of income,
  of influence,
  of fame across the sea.

But almost as quickly as these thoughts rise up
  in my mind,
  another takes their place.

> *Rejoice, . . . that the trial of your faith,*
> *being much more precious than of gold . . .*
> *might be found unto praise and honour and glory*
> *at the appearing of Jesus Christ.*

And I realize that this is proof.
He *is* changing me.
If this had happened only a few months ago
  I would have been distressed beyond words,
  perhaps even in despair.
But now I can honestly say that I feel only joy
  that my Lord lets me say "Thy will be done."
The sense of His loving-kindness to me
  is overwhelming.

EVERY JOY OR TRIAL

1

Switzerland called to me again with a voice I could
  not resist.
In August I returned in the company of my niece
  Constance Crane.
Elizabeth, Margaret, and Bessie joined us
  for some of our Alpine adventures.

I'm afraid I was rather idle the first month.
But in September, I discovered
  that there was plenty of time for both leisure and work.
It was as if a month's rest had given my mind
  a kind of spring cleaning.
I felt like I could start afresh,
  and writing became my first priority each day.
I made wonderful progress
  on my short devotional works for children,
  Little Pillows and *Morning Bells*.
By the end of my stay I had finished both manuscripts.

2

Working on my little books for children
   carried me back over the years to my own childhood
   and my own spiritual wrestlings with doubt.
I did not want other children to struggle as I had.
I didn't want them to lie awake at night,
   wondering if God had really forgiven them,
   or if they would ever know for certain that they were
   His child.

Little Pillows actually began one night
   when my niece was staying in my home.
I tucked her into bed and asked,
   "Shall I give you a little pillow?"

She sat up and looked at the pillow under her head.
"I already have one, Auntie."

"This is a different kind of pillow.
Not a pillow for your head, but a pillow for your heart.
It's a little word from God for you to rest on tonight."

And I gave her a verse of Scripture that night
   and the next.
One night she waited up for me for quite a while,
   not wanting to go to sleep without her little pillow.

And so I realized other children too
   might need these little pillows for their hearts
   each night.
Pillows like . . .

   Come unto me. (Matthew 11:28)

   I have loved you, saith the Lord. (Malachi 1:2)

   O Lord, Thou knowest. (Jeremiah 15:15)

With just a few words of explanation,
  children can understand the great truths
  of the Scriptures.
How might my childhood have been different
  if someone had given my heart a little pillow
  each night?

3

I found that everywhere I went,
  God brought people across my path,
  people hungry for His truth.
One day it was a laboring man who paused
  to drink at a stream where I was seated
  working on a poem.
I gave him a book, which he began reading
  there and then,
  and we had a wonderful talk.
We were joined eventually by his children,
  and by the time the morning was over,
  I had done little work on my poem,
  but had enjoyed the morning twice as much
  as if I had composed a masterpiece.

Not every hungry soul was so courteous.
Another day it was the keeper of a little inn
  in a village where I stopped for the night.
The tall, rough girl pointed me to a hard bench
  in a dirty room not meant for sitting.
"You can have a room when it's ready
  and not before," she told me
  and slammed the door.
I sat there for an hour, and the sky began to darken.

Finally she showed me to my room,
   a bit cleaner, thankfully, with a bed of barley straw
   and only a bolster for a pillow.

As I was preparing for bed,
   she rapped sharply on the door.
"Are you going to burn the candle all night?
How soon are you going to put it out?
You'll burn it all away!"

I swallowed my pride
   and answered as meekly as possible,
   "It shall be put out in a few minutes."
That night I prayed that God would let me speak
   with her
   next morning at breakfast.

She was still out of sorts in the morning.
She banged about the kitchen,
   gruffly informing me
   that I could not have coffee till it was made.
I took a deep breath.
"Lord, give me patience,"
   I whispered,
   and I sat outside until she called me.

"May I have some butter with my bread?"
I asked as she shoved a loaf toward me on the table.

"Butter? There is none."

I felt the right moment had come.
I met her angry eyes
   and made my voice gentle.
"You are not happy.
I know you are not."

Her eyes widened in a startled look.
Then her face crumpled.
She made a desperate effort not to cry.
I spoke openly to her of Jesus,
    and I gave her a French tract called
    "A Savior for You."

She slipped it into the pocket of her apron.
"I promise I'll read it, miss.
And thank you, oh, thank you."

It was worth all the discomfort of my stay
    for that one grateful look in her eyes.

4

I returned from Switzerland in perfect health
    and spent some time with the Cranes.
Before my journey home to Leamington,
    I met with a young woman at the request
    of my sister Maria.
I was fatigued and feared I could not manage it.
But the woman seemed comforted by our talk,
    and I was glad I had made the effort.

However, I caught a fever on the homeward journey.
I will not forget the misery of that train ride.
Dull headaches, sickness, chills, and shivering.

Upon my arrival at home,
    I had a full-blown case of typhoid fever.
Through a fog of pain and agony,
    I was able to hear God's promise to me,
    even when I could not quite see His face.
"I will never leave you."

I knew a case of typhoid often led to death.
And yet I could not think of death as a dark valley.
Rather I thought of it as going up,
    up a high hill to a bright golden gate,
    and waiting for it to open to me.
Waiting to see the face of my King.

5

It was during this illness that I wrote another hymn,
    one that later became more widely known than others.
I called it "Perfect Peace."
Many know it as "Like a River Glorious."

I have spent most of my life near rivers.
The River Severn in Worcester,
    the Rhine in Germany,
    all those lovely mountain torrents in Switzerland.
There is something very powerful
    and very peaceful about them.

Like a river glorious
Is God's perfect peace,
Over all victorious
In its bright increase.
Perfect—yet it floweth
Fuller every day;
Perfect—yet it groweth
Deeper all the way.

Stayed upon Jehovah,
Hearts are fully blest.
Finding, as He promised,
Perfect peace and rest.

Hidden in the hollow
Of His blessed hand,
Never foe can follow,
Never traitor stand.
Not a surge of worry,
Not a shade of care,
Not a blast of hurry
Touch the spirit there.

Every joy or trial
Falleth from above,
Traced upon our dial
By the Sun of Love.
We may trust Him fully
All for us to do;
They who trust Him wholly,
Find Him wholly true.

6

Thanks to the prayers of many,
    I survived the fever.
I even survived a relapse the following year.
My sister and mother and our servants cared for me
    in the family home at Leamington,
    and I also spent weeks with my sisters at Winterdyne
    and Oakhampton.

For the most part, I was unable to write.
Yet I thought often about the words
    of my consecration hymn.
Though my pen could not write verse,
    I could dictate letters of encouragement to friends.

Though I could not sing or lead a choir,
  I could pray for those who prayed for me.
Though I could not teach a Bible class
  in my drawing room,
  I could read God's Word to family members
  and servants.
I could still be "all for Jesus," even on a sickbed.

As the year 1875 mellowed into autumn,
  and the leaves began to deepen into brighter hues,
  I felt the cool refreshment of the autumn days.
I got out of bed,
  wrote for an hour or two a day,
  and even attended some church services
  and meetings of the Young Women's
  Christian Association.

It had been the most precious year of my life.
All the suffering had been worth it
  to prove for myself
  the truth of His words:

  When thou passest through the waters,
  I will be with thee.

7

In the year 1876 a different trial came.
Once again it was a letter that brought the news.
The hymnal I had worked on with Mr. Snepp,
  Songs of Grace and Glory, was being printed.
I had added harmonies to many of the tunes,
  and some of my own texts and music were included.
I was so glad my part in the hymnal was finished.
I was so eager to be on to another project,
  one of my own choosing.

But the letter told me there had been a fire at the printer's.
"Messrs. Henderson's premises were burned down
  this morning about four o'clock."
They were not yet certain of the extent of the damage
  to the plates for the hymnal.
It would be many days before the debris
  had cooled enough for them to know.

Weeks later, more news arrived.
The entire hymnal project had been
  completely destroyed in the flames,
  even the manuscript copy.

I had not saved copies of everything
  as I had been doing early in the composition process.
Most of my later work was just gone.
A whole winter's labor lost.

I dropped to my knees beside my writing desk.

  Every joy or trial falleth from above.

"Oh, Father, just like my illness,
  this too is from Your hand.
I know that."

  Take my intellect and use
  Every power as Thou wilt choose.

"I know I have been impatient
  to get on with work of my own choosing
  rather than willingly accepting the work You have
  for me.
It seems such drudgery to go back
  and do this work all over again, Father.
But please give me patience
  and help me to rejoice in Your plan for me."

It was a hard lesson.
But He gave me such gracious encouragement.
Work He chooses for me is never a waste of time.

I COULD NOT DO
WITHOUT THEE

1

My Dear Elizabeth,
To think that you are going to India!
It strikes me as wonderful that God
   in His providence
   lays different parts of His work on different hearts.
I have always wanted to be a missionary.
But the Lord has always closed the door
   because of my health.
I pray that your way will be made very clear,
   and that He will set before you an open door.

2

I would miss my friend Elizabeth,
   but I knew the Lord had different work for me to do
   at home in England.
So I threw myself into that work,
   as much as my health and strength would allow.

One week the Lord seemed to send blessing after blessing.

I was asked to sing at a women's meeting
at the YWCA one evening.
Many shook my hand and thanked me for singing.
Another day I visited an infirmary
where I sang and spoke to many who were sick
and suffering.
One woman trusted Christ,
and another told me my words had lifted her
straight up into the sunlight.

I'm not sure how it happened,
but by the end of the week I realized
there had been too much of *me* in all that I did,
and not enough of Jesus.

And I was so ashamed.
I sank down on my bed and let my face drop
into my hands.
I had failed in consecration, I, who had written the
"Consecration Hymn."
I had failed to live in the light of my own prayer.

Take my voice, and let me sing
Always, only, for my King.

At the next meeting of the YWCA,
I knew I could not sing.
So I had copies of my "Consecration Hymn" printed.
I left my name off
and in its place I drew a blank line on every copy.
I asked the young women to pray the words back
to God.
And then I asked each to write her own name
in the blank.

At the end of that meeting,
  I felt there had been *real* blessing.

3

Sometimes at meetings or on visits,
  I gave out leaflets I had written.
One of my leaflets was based on my hymn
  "I Could Not Do Without Thee."
How I longed for others
  to feel how much they needed the Savior,
  even as I did.

> *I could not do without Thee,*
> *O Saviour of the lost!*
> *Whose precious blood redeemed me,*
> *At such tremendous cost.*
> *Thy righteousness, Thy pardon,*
> *Thy precious blood must be*
> *My only hope and comfort,*
> *My glory and my plea!*
>
> *I could not do without Thee!*
> *I cannot stand alone,*
> *I have no strength or goodness,*
> *No wisdom of my own.*
> *But Thou, beloved Saviour,*
> *Art all in all to me;*
> *And weakness will be power,*
> *If leaning hard on Thee.*
>
> *I could not do without Thee!*
> *For years are fleeting fast,*
> *And soon, in solemn loneliness,*
> *The river must be passed.*

But Thou wilt never leave me,
And, though the waves roll high,
I know Thou wilt be near me,
And whisper, "It is I."

4

For many years I had pressed my sister Maria
    to go to Switzerland with me.
I knew she needed the refreshment.
Finally I won her over.
In July of 1876 we went on our delightful journey.

I decided to write a hymn in French,
    Seulement pour Toi.
Of course a hymn called "Only *for* Thee"
    must also include the idea of "only *by* Thee."
We wanted the many friends we met
    in the places we stayed
    to know that they must come to God
    not by a church, not by their good works,
    but only by Jesus Christ.

And we sang it everywhere.
In impromptu concerts for our host families,
    while sitting outside admiring the mountain views,
    while riding the coach from one town to the next.
Even our driver joined in with his hearty bass voice.
We taught it to anyone who would listen.
Maria even took it to the Roman Catholic priest
    to ask him if my French wording were correct.
Imagine taking a Protestant hymn to a Catholic priest.

And yet he was gracious,
   and we trust the Lord spoke truth to his heart.

5

One day in Champèry,
   I met the Baroness Helga von Cramm.
What a lovely artist.
How skillfully she painted the snow
   on the Alpine heights,
   overshadowed by clouds.
And all her exquisite drawings of Alpine flowers!
Every picture was a poem in itself.

One day over tea it was decided.
We would combine our arts to produce some cards.
Her paintings and my poems.
She had wanted to do some work for Jesus
   and was thrilled at the prospect.

6

In September I got caught in a thunderstorm.
I was soaked through before I could get to shelter.
Aching and feverish,
   I saw as if through a dense fog
   Maria sitting by my bed, wiping my brow
   with a cool cloth.
I asked her to take down a poem.

   I take this pain, Lord Jesus,
   From Thine own hand,

The strength to bear it bravely
Thou wilt command.

'Tis Thy dear hand, O Saviour,
That presseth sore,
The hand that bears the nail-prints
For evermore.

7

We left Switzerland in October,
  once I had strength enough to travel.
It was on the return journey that I had the idea
  for another book.

England's early dark had settled down around us.
We had just passed Oxford Station.
Maria and I had been dozing
  to the rhythm of the train wheels
  clacking over the tracks.

But I suddenly sat up,
  seeing it all flash through my mind—
  title, theme, outline of chapters.

"I'll call it *My King!*" I exclaimed.

"What, Frances?"

"My book.
I found a verse the other day in 2 Samuel 14.
A little pillow of sorts.
The note on verse 17 in the margin of my Bible
  made me think of it in a different way.
A woman said to King David, 'The word of my lord
  the king
  shall now be for rest.'

"You know, the same can be said of Jesus,
  the Son of David.
His words give me rest and comfort,
  not just for myself, but for others.
And now I know what I'll do.
I will write thirty-one chapters,
  one for each day of the month,
  about the King's words."

I could hardly wait to get home
  to get started.
The words were ready to pour out through my pen
  from a fountain springing up inside me.

I worked quickly.
I worked between hours of pain
  and hours of sleep.
The Lord helped me.
How could I do without Him?
My book seemed to write itself.

It was the first of five little books of devotional thoughts about my King Jesus.
I called them my Royal Books.

TAKE WHAT THOU WILT

1

Dear Elizabeth,
How curiously your path and mine have diverged;
  you're going to do great things for God,
  and I am able for less and less.
I had hoped to do one Bible class this winter
  and to lead the choir,
  but I think I will be staying much at home.
I know God will give you peace in your work,
  and He will give me peace in my waiting.

2

Even when I could do little else,
  I wrote or dictated letters.
There was a young friend I was troubled about
  because I saw in him the doubt and fear,
  the dissatisfaction
I had felt in my own childhood.

I wrote him several letters
　　urging him to come out on the Lord's side.

I hear you are going back to school on Thursday.
Are you to go back doubtful, uneasy, fearful, alone?
Or is it to be going back with Jesus,
　　safe and happy in Him?
It is a grand thing to start out early
　　and be on the Lord's side all along.

To another young man I wrote:

I can't bear those who might be even officers,
　　let alone recruits, in His army
　　to be contented to stay at home
　　and fight their own little private battles
　　for their own ends
　　and the cause of the Redeemer
　　left to take its chance!

3

The words to a new hymn grew in my mind
　　with these letters to young people.
More than a hymn, it was a challenge.
A challenge to take up arms
　　and join the King's army.
I wrote it as a series of questions
　　followed by a response.
I called it simply "On the Lord's Side."

　　Who is on the Lord's side?
　　Who will serve the King?

Who will be His helpers,
Other lives to bring?
Who will leave the world's side?
Who will face the foe?
Who is on the Lord's side?
Who for Him will go?

By Thy call of mercy,
By Thy grace divine,
We are on the Lord's side;
Saviour, we are Thine.

Jesus, Thou hast bought us,
Not with gold or gem,
But with Thine own life-blood,
For Thy diadem.
With Thy blessing filling
Each who comes to Thee,
Thou hast made us willing,
Thou hast made us free.

By Thy grand redemption,
By Thy grace divine,
We are on the Lord's side;
Saviour, we are Thine.

Fierce may be the conflict,
Strong may be the foe,
But the King's own army
None can overthrow.
Round His standard ranging,
Victory is secure,
For His truth unchanging
Makes the triumph sure.

Joyfully enlisting
By Thy grace divine,

We are on the Lord's side;
Saviour, we are Thine.

4

Mama was ill, and it pained me
  to see my stepmother in such pain.
I think it is easier for me to go through pain myself
  than to watch someone else try to bear it.
I prayed she would have more grace,
  more tenderness,
  more comfort from God
  whenever she felt more pain.

Mama opened her eyes as I knelt by her bed
  the morning of May 26, 1878.
She had been lying still for so long,
  unaware of all around her.
But this day she looked at me
  and recognized my face
  and smiled sweetly.
It was her last smile.
Later she passed into the presence of Jesus,
  where she could rest from pain,
  where she would exchange suffering for glory.

5

Maria and I felt that the time had come
  to clean out the family home in Leamington
  and go elsewhere.

But the many details involved in sorting
   through our things
   collected through years of living
   were overwhelming.
During this time the Lord showed me
   one more little step
   that I could take for Him.
I had so much jewelry that I did not need
   and a jewelry box fit for a countess.

One morning I opened the lid
   and the sun gleamed on the gemstones
   making prisms dance on my bedroom walls.
The words to my "Consecration Hymn"
   sang through my mind.

   Take my silver and my gold;
   Not a mite would I withhold.

I decided to pack the jewelry
   and give it to the church to be sold
   and the money used for missionary work.
I kept only a few keepsakes from my parents,
   my locket with my only portrait
   of my dear niece Evelyn,
   now in heaven,
   and the two rings I wear always
   in memory of her.

What joy to obey the Lord
   in this small matter.
I had no idea I had so much jewelry,
   nearly enough to open my own shop.
Gemstone rings, cameo brooches, pendant necklaces.

I laid them all out on the bed
   and wrapped each piece in paper.
I never packed a box with such pleasure.

6

I stare around me at the empty room,
   my room in our Leamington home
   where I spent so many countless hours
   writing, reading,
   lying on my sickbed,
   talking to friends and family members.
Soon I will close the door on this room for the last time.

Maria pokes her head in the doorway.
"Are you almost ready, Frances?"

"Yes, I'm ready. I was just . . . remembering."

"You're not having second thoughts about our move?"

"Oh, no. I know the Lord has shown us that it's time,
   but I was just thinking of all that He did for me here.
Not just the work He allowed me to do
   and the illnesses He brought me through,
   but also what He did in my heart."

I look around. "There is where I read the letter
   from my publishers in America
   telling me their business had failed.
I thought my prospects in America were ended.
But look what God has done.
I have many American publishers asking for my work,
   more work than I am able to do."

Maria nodded. "And there is the bed
   where you lay desperately ill those two times.
I thought I would lose you,
   but I'm so glad God has spared your life."

"My times are in His hand, Maria.
I just long to be useful to Him
   till the very end.
Do you suppose we will ever really
   have a home of our own again?"

"Perhaps not, my dear,
   but we have each other."

I cross the room,
   embrace my sister with tears in my eyes.
"And for that I'm unspeakably grateful.
God is so good to us."

7

After closing up our home,
   I traveled and visited friends.
And God did give my sister and me a home.
In October of 1878 I joined Maria
   in the small white house she had taken
   on a headland of Caswell Bay called the Mumbles
   in Swansea, South Wales.

It was not grand.
Neither of us wanted a castle,
   but just a happy little nest.

It had a pretty garden in front
    with a sea of blue forget-me-nots
    in summer.

It was rather bare,
    but I went to work right away
    with hammer and nails
    and some pretty cloth
    and transformed our packing boxes
    into tables and music stands.
I built a stand for my piano
    and placed the sofa with a view of the sunsets.
I set up my own desk
    with my books and papers
    and my American typewriter
    and made it all ready for the work
    I would do in the year 1879.

8

The sea air had refreshed me by this time,
  and I felt rested and well.
I enjoyed ocean walks
  and scrambles on the cliffs.
I watched the ships sail in and out
  over the foam-crested waves.
I watched the lovely sea anemones
  basking in the tide pools.
I climbed the stairs to the top of the lighthouse
  and learned all that the keeper could tell me
  about the winds and the waves,
  the stars and the sea.

To think that my Lord
  is master of all His creation.
Sometimes I watched storms arise at sea,
  and I thought how wind and wave
  obeyed His will while He walked on earth.

I composed melodies to some of my poems,
  and I wrote some new hymns.

9

Here is one of the hymns I wrote that year,
  November 1878, looking out over the shores
  of Caswell Bay.
I called it "What Thou Wilt."

Do what Thou wilt! Yes, only do
What seemeth good to Thee:
Thou art so loving, wise, and true,
It must be best for me.

Send what Thou wilt; or beating shower,
Soft dew, or brilliant sun;
Alike in still and stormy hour,
My Lord, Thy will be done.

Teach what Thou wilt; and make me learn
Each lesson full and sweet,
And deeper things of God discern
While sitting at Thy feet.

Say what Thou wilt; and let each word
My quick obedience win;
Let loyalty and love be stirred
To deeper glow within.

Give what Thou wilt; for then I know
I shall be rich indeed;
My King rejoices to bestow
Supply for every need.

Take what Thou wilt, beloved Lord,
For I have all in Thee!
My own exceeding great reward,
Thou, Thou Thyself shalt be!

I AM TRUSTING THEE, LORD JESUS

1

I came to the home at the Mumbles for rest.
Yet rest was hard to find.
There was so much work to be done.
Publisher proofs to read and correct,
   letters to answer,
   new writing to do,
   and even a Bible study to lead.
I invited the people in the neighboring cottages
   to come to our home for Bible readings.
Week by week, the room was full.
The meetings continued till Christmas
   and brought me great joy.

2

I was given a "journal of mercies" at the beginning
   of 1879.
I began writing down one mercy from God
   at the close of every day.

I learned to see even small things as mercies.
A night of unbroken sleep,
  freedom from pain,
  fresh air, spring sunshine,
  a gospel sermon at church,
  a beautiful sunset.
One day I wrote that I was beginning
  to develop a habit of trust.
Taking God's mercies from His hand each day
  and learning to be grateful
  for whatever He sends.
This is what it means to trust.

3

In March I finished another book,
  Kept for the Master's Use.
I took each verse of my "Consecration Hymn"
  and wrote my thoughts about how to apply it.
Letters have told me
  that many have been blessed by this hymn,
  and I thought a book would encourage them
  to go on with the Lord
  to higher and higher ground.
How I prayed over that book.
Sometimes instead of writing,
  I would spend a day in prayer.
Knowing my work will go out
  to tens of thousands
  is a serious and humbling thing,
  and I needed God's help for my task.

This need for prayer before all my work
   led me to write the hymn "Lord, Speak to Me."

   Lord, speak to me, that I may speak
   In living echoes of Thy tone;
   As Thou hast sought, so let me seek
   Thy erring children, lost, and lone.

   O lead me, Lord, that I may lead
   The wandering and the wavering feet;
   O feed me, Lord, that I may feed
   Thy hungering ones with manna sweet.

   O teach me, Lord, that I may teach
   The precious things Thou dost impart;
   And wing my words, that they may reach
   The hidden depths of many a heart.

4

Around Easter time I worked on a delightful project
   with the school children who lived around us.
I told them I would give each child a Bible
   who could say Isaiah 53
   from memory.
To see their earnest faces
   as they spoke those holy words
   about the one who carried their griefs
   and bore their sorrows
   was like the taste of honey
   to my heart.
I did not excuse a single mistake.
But I did give many a second try.

5

Spring brought visits from friends.
How wonderful to see my dear Elizabeth Clay
   in Wales for a short time
   on her furlough from India.
I reveled in the details of her work;
   I could have listened to her stories for hours.

I wonder if I will ever be able to go to India myself.
I do hope I can someday learn
   to write in the Eastern languages,
   perhaps even a song for the Indian people
   about my King.

Mr. and Mrs. Ira Sankey also visited from America
   that spring.
Mr. Sankey, another hymnwriter,
   and his dear wife have encouraged me
   in the writing of my own hymns.
We spoke much
   about our hope in Christ
   and that bright city to which we are going one day.

And my friend the Baroness Helga von Cramm
   came in May.
We sat together on the sands
   while she sketched the lighthouse
   towering over the bay.
We spoke of our common faith
   in Christ, our light
   and our strong tower.

6

It is May, and once again I am too weary
and too ill to leave my bed.
I am very cozily settled here
with my two pet kittens, Dot and Trot,
tumbling about on the duvet.

Maria has arranged some of Helga's pictures
where I can see them from the bed.
The pictures of those high rugged Alps
with their snow-covered peaks
take my thoughts away up there,
away from my pain.

I feel almost certain that this time is different.
I do not think I shall recover.
It will not be long now,
and I will see my King face to face.
God's will is delicious.
He makes no mistakes.

"Are you afraid, Frances?" Maria asks me,
her anxious eyes intent on my face.

I smile at her. "Why should I be?
Jesus said 'It is finished.'
And what was His precious blood shed for?
I trust that."

EPILOGUE

Frances Ridley Havergal died on June 3, 1879. She was forty-two years old. Her last complete sentences to the family members gathered around her bed were: "There, now it is all over. Blessed rest." She died trying to sing, her radiant face lifted, her eyes looking up.

She was buried in the Astley churchyard within sight of the place of her birth. Her tomb is beside her father's. The inscription on her tombstone reads:

FRANCES RIDLEY HAVERGAL
YOUNGEST DAUGHTER OF THE REV. W. H. HAVERGAL
AND JANE HIS WIFE
Born at Astley Rectory 14th December 1836
Died at Caswell Bay Swansea 3rd June 1879 Aged 42
By her writings in prose and verse she being dead yet speaketh
The blood of Jesus Christ His Son cleanseth us from all sin I John 1:7

Found in her Bible after her death were the words to her personal favorite of all the hymns she had written. "I Am Trusting Thee, Lord Jesus" was written in Switzerland in 1874.

I am trusting Thee, Lord Jesus,
Trusting only Thee;
Trusting Thee for full salvation,
Great and free.

I am trusting Thee for pardon;
At Thy feet I bow,
For Thy grace and tender mercy,
Trusting now.

I am trusting Thee for cleansing
In the crimson flood;
Trusting Thee to make me holy
By Thy blood.

I am trusting Thee to guide me;
Thou alone must lead!
Every day and hour supplying
All my need.

I am trusting Thee for power:
Thine can never fail!
Words which Thou thyself shalt give me,
Must prevail.

I am trusting Thee, Lord Jesus;
Never let me fall!
I am trusting Thee for ever,
And for all.

SOURCES

Budgen, Pamela D. *Ever, Only, All for Thee: Frances Ridley Havergal: Glimpses of Her Life and Writings.* Battle Ground, WA: Christian Resources, 2007.

Cook, Faith. "'In Full and Glad Surrender': Frances Ridley Havergal." *Our Hymn Writers and Their Hymns.* Darlington, England: Evangelical Press, 2005.

Darlow, T. H. *Frances Ridley Havergal: A Saint of God.* New York: Revell, 1927.

Havergal, Frances Ridley. *Little Pillows and Morning Bells.* Birmingham, AL: Solid Ground Christian Books, reprinted from the 1883 edition of *Little Pillows* (Dutton, NY) and the 1880 edition of *Morning Bells* (Anson Randolph, NY).

Havergal, Frances Ridley. *The Poetical Works of Frances Ridley Havergal.* New York: E. P. Dutton, 1888. Primary source of poetry and song lyrics in this biography.

Havergal, Maria V. G. *Memorials of Frances Ridley Havergal.* London: Nisbet, 1880.

James, Sharon. "Frances Ridley Havergal (1836–1879)." *In Trouble and in Joy: Four Women Who Lived for God.* Darlington, England: Evangelical Press, 2003.